MADELEINE
ALBRIGHT

MADELEINE ALBRIGHT

Michael Burgan

The Millbrook Press
Brookfield, Connecticut

I would like to thank the following people and institutions for their valuable assistance: the Western History/Genealogy Department, Denver Public Library; Blake Smith and Professor Ronald Lieber, Georgetown University; Susan Jay; and the Office of Public Affairs, Wellesley College. A special thank you to Amy Shields and the staff at the Millbrook Press, and to all the history teachers who have inspired me over the years.

Photographs courtesy of Sygma: pp. 10 (© Wally McNamee), 26 (© Illka Uimonen), 35 (© Brooks Kraft), 39 (© Illka Uimonen), 122 (© Illka Uimonen); Corbis: pp. 22, 77; AP/Wide World Photos: pp. 47, 65, 101, 113; Corbis-Bettmann: pp. 81, 116

Library of Congress Cataloging-in-Publication Data
Burgan, Michael.
Madeleine Albright / Michael Burgan.
p.   cm.
Includes index.
Summary: A biography of the former U.S. ambassador to the United Nations, from her childhood in war-torn Prague, Czechoslovakia, to her appointment as the first woman Secretary of State.
ISBN 0-7613-0367-7 (lib. bdg.)
1. Albright, Madeleine Korbel—Juvenile literature. 2. Women cabinet officers—United States—Biography—Juvenile literature. 3. Cabinet officers—United States—Biography—Juvenile literature. 4. United Nations—Officials and employees—Biography—Juvenile literature. 5. Ambassadors—United States—Biography—Juvenile literature. [1. Albright, Madeleine Korbel. 2. Cabinet officers. 3. Ambassadors. 4. Women—Biography.] I. Title.
E840.8.A37B87   1998
327.73'0092—dc21
[B]   98-6880   CIP   AC

Published by The Millbrook Press, Inc.
2 Old New Milford Road
Brookfield, CT   06804

CONTENTS

MADELEINE
ALBRIGHT

CHAPTER I

*"We must be the authors
of the history of our age"*

PREPARED STATEMENT TO CONGRESS, 1/8/97

On January 23, 1997, members of the media and congressional leaders gathered in the Oval Office of the White House. Just three days before, America had celebrated President Bill Clinton's second inauguration. Now, President Clinton was the master of ceremonies for another swearing in.

In the center of the room, with her family beside her, stood Madeleine Albright. A small American eagle brooch was pinned to her navy-blue dress. President Clinton stepped to the microphone, introducing Albright as America's new secretary of state—the first woman to hold the office and the highest-ranking woman ever in the federal government.

When Albright considered the line of great figures she was joining, she was struck with a sense of awe. Her predecessors included some of America's finest political thinkers, such as former presidents James Madison and Thomas Jefferson, who also was the country's first secretary of state. John Marshall, one

Secretary of State Madeleine Albright

of the greatest chief justices of the Supreme Court, was another who served in that position. So had such important congressional leaders as Henry Clay and Daniel Webster.

Along with trying to meet the standards set by her predecessors, Albright was undertaking one of the most important jobs in a president's cabinet. The secretary of state advises the president on foreign affairs and travels the world representing the U.S. government. The secretary also oversees the country's worldwide diplomatic staff. In the event of an emergency, the secretary of state is fifth in line for the presidency. (Albright, however, as a foreign-born citizen, could not assume the presidency.)

Henry Stimson, who held the position under President Herbert Hoover, said that no secretary of state can "fail to feel the extraordinary responsibility he carries for service to the country and its peace."[1]

The secretary of state's responsibilities continue to grow. America is the economic and military superpower of the world. The secretary has to articulate the president's foreign policy to the American public and Congress, mobilizing support for programs such as a potential military mission or financial aid to countries in need.

Although America is a world leader, it has always had a strong isolationist bent. Some politicians have sought to keep the country away from the world's problems. George Washington, in his farewell address to the nation, set the tone for this kind of sentiment. He warned America to "steer clear of permanent alliances with any portion of the foreign world."[2]

Today, however, in a world "shrunk" by satellite communications, the Internet, and high-speed travel, isolationism is not a real option for American foreign policy, and Albright never supported that view. She, along with President Clinton, believes that America is the world's "indispensable nation." And she had prepared for the demands of guiding America's foreign policy at her former job as U.S. ambassador to the United Nations.

Four years earlier, in 1992, Clinton had named Albright to the UN post and also made her a member of his cabinet. The president trusted Albright's political instincts and knowledge of foreign affairs. She quickly became a highly visible spokesperson for the administration's goals. And she never shied away from a TV camera or a reporter's questions, offering compact, no-nonsense observations.

Her candor as UN ambassador led one magazine to call Albright "Clinton's blunt instrument" in foreign affairs.[3] For example, in 1994, Iraq complained about the continuing UN economic embargo put in place after the Persian Gulf War. Tariq Aziz, Iraq's UN ambassador, said the country had improved its international manners, but just two weeks before, Iraq had once again sent troops near the Kuwaiti border. "Talk is cheap," Albright snapped. "Actions are the coins of the realm."[4]

Another time at the United Nations, when discussing Haiti's military government, Albright said, "They have created a puppet show and called it a government."[5] Albright's terse words sometimes raised eyebrows, but she also won praise for avoiding the evasive language common in diplomatic circles. "I tell it like it is," she often reminded reporters.[6] Albright's tough talk also won her the respect of the person who mattered most—Bill Clinton.

After Clinton won a second term in November 1996, Secretary of State Warren Christopher stepped down. The buzz about Albright's being offered his job had started even before the election. On December 5, Clinton confirmed it, introducing his new national-security team. At this press conference, she immediately showed her ease in the spotlight, joking to Warren Christopher, "I can only hope that my heels can fill your shoes."[7] Albright then turned serious, focusing on the message she wanted to bring in her new job. "If we are to master events," she said, "rather than be mastered by them, we must be forward looking in our thinking and flexible in our tactics. But we need not—and must not—diverge from the core values of democracy and respect for human dignity that have long guided our nation."[8]

In the weeks after Albright's nomination, reporters and political experts discussed the significance of her appointment. There were the obvious comments about its historic nature—first female secretary of state—and speculation about her performance in her new role. But before Albright could officially start the job, she had to be confirmed by the Senate. The Senate Democrats wholeheartedly supported Albright's nomination. But the Republicans controlled the Senate, and they would decide Albright's fate.

Leading the hearings before Albright's confirmation vote was Senator Jesse Helms, chairman of the Senate Foreign Relations Committee. Helms, a Republican from North Carolina, was known for his ultraconservative views. He had never been a supporter of the United Nations and resented the verbal abuse that he felt America endured there. But, to the surprise of some observers, Helms welcomed Albright's appointment. He called her a "tough and courageous" lady.[9] Most important, to a senator's way of thinking, Albright understood that Congress has a role to play in shaping foreign policy. With Helms's endorsement, Albright was guaranteed a smooth confirmation process.

The confirmation hearing was held on January 8, 1997. The members of the Foreign Relations Committee praised Albright, calling her a role model for the country. They also applauded her strong condemnation of the world's dictatorships, including Iraq, Cuba, and Myanmar (formerly Burma). In the past, some Republicans had questioned the doctrine that Albright urged at the United Nations, which called for the United States to use its troops for humanitarian missions around the world—often when America had no vital interest at stake. But, despite her controversial views, Albright was the star that day.

Albright outlined for the senators her broad goals as secretary, including strengthening America's ties with its European allies and promoting security and prosperity in Asia. She also hoped to use the State Department to address global environmental issues, the status of the world's women and children, and international drug smuggling. Albright left no doubt about America's ability to confront so many problems: "We are doers."[10] Less than two weeks later, on January 22, the Senate voted 99–0 to confirm Albright as secretary of state.

The next day, with President Clinton finishing his introduction, Vice President Gore was ready to administer the oath of office. Within moments, Madeleine Albright was the 63rd secretary of state of the United States. Albright prepared to make her first comments in her new position. Ever since her appointment to the United Nations, Albright had impressed people with the strength of her words and values. With President Clinton by her side, she again focused on strength:

> *America is strong, our principles are ascendant and our leadership both respected and welcome in most corners of the world. But if we are complacent or timid or unwilling to look beyond our borders, our citizens will not prosper and the framework of American leadership and the foundation of American security we have built could crumble with twenty-first century speed. We cannot allow that to happen. We must not shy from the mantle of leadership, nor hesitate to defend our interests, nor fail in our commitments, nor diverge from the principles that have defined, elevated, and sustained our nation for more than 200 years.*[11]

The day after the ceremony, Secretary Albright attended meetings and interviews devoted to her goals as secretary. She held her first news conference and discussed a wide range of topics, including U.S. relations with China and Cuba, and Iran's and Iraq's support of terrorism. Albright ended the day with an appearance on the TV program "Larry King Live."

A frequent guest on the Larry King show, Albright displayed her usual ease in front of the TV camera. She said how happy she was to be on the program, since one of her major goals as secretary was to educate Americans about her role and America's foreign policy. For fifty years, the country's international interests were shaped by the Cold War, a struggle of values between America's democracy and the communism of the Soviet Union. "We were the good guys and they were the bad guys," the secretary said. "Now what we have to try to figure out and explain to people [is] what the threats are against our way of life and how to protect ourselves from that."[12]

But Albright didn't talk only about her goals for the future. She stressed how honored and proud she was to have her new position. "I never even thought about the possibility of being secretary of state before, because who would have ever thought that a girl who arrived from Czechoslovakia at age eleven could become secretary of state of the most powerful country in the world."[13]

Albright's early years in her homeland truly shaped the woman who would become the secretary of state of the United States. She may have been only eleven when she arrived in America, but her life had already taken fascinating turns—and dangerous ones, as well.

CHAPTER 2

"My parents are the bravest people I've ever known"

TIME, 2/17/97

Madeleine Albright's story, like most Americans', was an immigrant's story. She and her family fled Czechoslovakia in 1948, when a Communist government backed by the Soviet Union came to power. But even before that, Albright and her family had faced terror, fleeing the Nazi Germans after their takeover of Czechoslovakia. Her experience with dictatorships gave Albright a keen appreciation of democracy; she would never take it for granted. And as she immersed herself in foreign affairs, first as a scholar, then as a diplomat, she believed America had to both promote and defend its democratic values around the world.

A city of grand churches and palaces, Prague straddles the Vltava River. This capital city of what was once Czechoslovakia (now two nations, the Czech Republic and Slovakia) was founded more than 1,000 years ago, and a castle dating from the twelfth century overlooks the city from the west bank of the river. Prague has been acclaimed as one of Europe's most beautiful cities.

Until the end of World War I, the Czechs lived under the domination of the Austro-Hungarian Empire. The empire was ruled by one of Europe's last great dynasties, the Hapsburgs. But the Great War had ended their reign, and the victorious French and British allies carved up the old empire and created new democratic states. The Czech-speaking lands of Moravia and Bohemia united with Slovakia to form one country, Czechoslovakia. For the first time in 300 years, the Czechs had their own government.

In the years after World War I, Czechoslovakia developed the strongest democratic government and one of the best economies in Central Europe. Prague offered many opportunities for talented young Czechs, and that's where Josef Korbel, Madeleine Albright's father, began his career.

The Korbel family came to the capital from Kysperk (now called Letohrad), a small town in Moravia. In 1933 the twenty-four-year-old Josef completed his degree in international law at Prague's Charles University, one of the best schools in Central Europe. He then briefly served in the army before entering the Czech diplomatic service.

In 1935, Korbel married his high school sweetheart, Mandula Spieglova. Shortly after, Korbel went to Belgrade, Yugoslavia, as a press attaché at the Czech embassy. Korbel made a good impression in his new job: "Energetic and gregarious, Korbel immediately became a valued member of Belgrade's intellectual and cultural aristocracy."[1]

The Korbels had their first child on May 15, 1937, a daughter they named Marie Jana. Although years later she would be called Madeleine, her family nickname was Madlenka. After Madlenka's birth in Prague, she and her mother joined Josef Korbel in Belgrade.

The Korbels were blessed with good fortune. But back in Prague, and throughout Central Europe, fear was building, fueled by the rise of Nazi Germany. As 1938 began, many Europeans felt the first rumblings of another world war.

The Allies, after World War I, had tried to guarantee that Germany would never threaten its neighbors again. However, most historians agree that the harsh conditions of the Versailles peace treaty struck Germany too hard. The Allies forced Germany to destroy most of its weapons, sacrifice territory, and make reparations—payments to the countries it had attacked during the war.

The treaty made most Germans angry, their pride punctured by the steep terms of peace. In the postwar period, Germany was hit with domestic chaos as well, as inflation ruined the economy and its new democratic government struggled to take hold. In the midst of these problems, many Germans welcomed a leader who would restore their national pride and bring order to everyday life. That man was Adolf Hitler.

Hitler led the National Socialists, a party that opposed communism and promoted German ethnic purity, which sounded benign but was actually based on a violent anti-Semitism. By 1933 Hitler's "Nazis" were Germany's largest political group, and Hitler was appointed the country's chancellor. Over the next five years, Hitler and the Nazis took control of the government, established a totalitarian regime, re-armed Germany, and began looking for other countries to dominate.

In March 1938, Hitler marched into Austria. For the most part, the Austrians, too, welcomed Nazi rule. Months later, Hitler began to eye the Sudetenland, a part of Czechoslovakia where 3 million German-speaking people lived. The Czechs watched warily as Hitler called their country a second-rate state and proclaimed brotherhood with the Germans in the Sudetenland. By August he was threatening war against Czechoslovakia.

France and Britain feared the Nazi military buildup and desire for other lands, but they also dreaded the prospect of another war. The two powers adopted a policy of appeasement: They would give Hitler what he wanted in Central Europe to avoid a conflict.

On September 29, 1938, representatives from France, Britain, Germany, and Italy met in Munich, Germany, to decide the fate of the Sudetenland. Czechoslovakia, an ally of France, was left out of the meeting; it had no say in its own future. The mood that day in Prague was somber, and the news from Munich made it more so.

France and Britain agreed to give Hitler almost everything he demanded. German troops would occupy the Sudetenland, and the region would be under German control. In the process, the Czechs would surrender a system of fortifications on their border with Germany, their sole defense from any future German attack.

In England, the Munich agreement brought cheers for the country's prime minister, Neville Chamberlain. He had been the driving force behind the agreement with Hitler. Returning from Munich, Chamberlain proudly asserted he had achieved "peace with honor." The French also welcomed the accord and the preservation of peace.

In Prague, however, a silent dread gripped the Czechs as they contemplated their future. On September 30, Premier Jan Syrovy gave a radio address, saying the country had to accept conditions that "in their mercilessness are unexampled in history."[2] Czechoslovakia had only two options: accept the Munich agreement or fight a potentially devastating war. In this case, war was not a viable solution. "We were abandoned," Syrovy said. "We stood entirely alone."

Less than three months later, Josef Korbel and his family returned from Belgrade to their fearful hometown. Tensions grew across Czechoslovakia as Hitler threatened to take over the rest of the country. Germans in Slovakia, Moravia, and Bohemia clamored for Nazi "protection" from the Czechs. Finally, on March 15, 1939, the Germans completed their domination of Czechoslovakia.

A strong wind whipped snow through Prague as German troops paraded down the city's ancient streets. Czechs of German descent greeted the troops, cheering and waving flags adorned with swastikas, the symbol of the Nazi Party. Adolph Hitler himself rode triumphantly into the city and spent the night at Hradcany, the ancient castle on Prague's western hill. Czechoslovakia's short life as an independent, democratic country was over.

For the Korbels, the days to follow were filled with panic and hasty planning. Josef Korbel's name

As Nazi troops roll into the town of Eger in October 1938, the faces of these Czech women show the wide range of emotions the invasion inspired—from enthusiastic to stoic to utter despair.

was on a list of people the Germans wanted to arrest; his close ties to the democratic government made him untrustworthy in Nazi eyes. Madlenka was not yet two years old, and her parents left her with various family members while they spent their nights in the homes of friends and prepared to flee Czechoslovakia.

Finally, the Korbels convinced the Germans to let them leave the country. "We managed to get the necessary Gestapo permission . . . about 5 o'clock in the evening," Mandula Korbel wrote many years later.

"And by 11 o'clock the same night, we all three were on a train to Belgrade with two small suitcases that we were able to pack in a hurry. That was the last time we saw our parents alive."[3]

The Korbels left behind their parents—Madlenka's grandparents—as they started a journey that took them first to Yugoslavia, then Greece, and finally to the safety of London. Other leading Czechs had already fled to the British capital, where they set up a government-in-exile. This democratic government far from home was the true Czech government, the refugees believed. One day the Nazis would fall, and the leaders would return to their freed homeland and resume power.

London, however, soon became a dangerous place for the Korbels—and the English as well—as Hitler continued to send his armies across Central Europe. On September 1, 1939, the Germans invaded Poland; this time the British and French could not ignore Hitler's aggression. Siding with Poland, the Allies fought back. World War II had begun.

Josef Korbel joined the Czech government-in-exile as the head of the information department. Using the facilities of the British Broadcasting Company, Korbel supervised radio shows beamed back to Czechoslovakia, designed to give the Czechs the truth about war and to keep their spirits high.

By September 1940, Hitler had control of most of Central and Western Europe, and he turned his attention to England. German planes flew over London, bombing the capital and forcing the Korbels and millions of others underground for safety.

To keep their spirits up during the German raids, the Korbel family sang songs in the bomb shelters. Years later, as secretary of state, Madeleine Albright reflected on her early childhood in England: "I remember the war distinctly. We were in London during the blitz. I remember what it was like to come out of the air raid shelter and see London bombed."[4] What young Madlenka saw was buildings blasted into rubble, double-decker buses resting in the craters of bombed-out streets, and fires that raged into the night.

Hoping to escape the worst of the raids, Josef Korbel moved his family out of the city into the suburbs, eventually settling in Walton-on-Thames. There, Albright later recalled, the family owned a steel table. "They said if your house was bombed, and you were under the table, you would survive. . . . We ate on the table and we slept under the table and we played around the table."[5]

Despite the air raids and the uncertainty of the situation in Czechoslovakia, the Korbels tried to lead a normal life. In October 1942, Madlenka's sister, Anna Katherine, was born. The Korbels' niece Dagmar also lived with the family when she was not at boarding school. Nine years older than Madlenka, Dagmar had vivid memories of her young cousin. "Madeleine was a very bright child, very bossy. . . . I didn't mind it when she bossed me around. It was fun. She is a born leader, you know."[6]

Madlenka went to school and learned to speak fluent English. Raised as a Roman Catholic, the young girl sometimes pretended she was a priest. Later, recalling this, Albright said, "I was already playing male roles."[7]

Madlenka also questioned her parents about life back home, and they told her about the glorious years of the 1920s and early 1930s, when Czechoslovakia had been free.

As World War II went on, Allied successes on the battlefield made it apparent that Czechoslovakia would regain its freedom. One American army, led by General George Patton, raced eastward across Europe, smashing the war-weary German forces. The Korbels listened in May 1945 as the radio broadcast news of Patton's triumphs. They also heard, however, that Patton had to stop before he reached Prague, so the Soviet Union's Red Army could liberate the city.

Between August 1939 and June 1941, the Soviets had a nonaggression pact with Germany—until the Nazis launched a sneak attack on the Communist country. During World War II the Soviets engaged German troops on the eastern front, driving back the invading Nazis. Their heroic fighting gave America and Britain time to launch an attack on Germany from the west. Now, in 1945, Soviet armies occupied most of Eastern Europe. Their presence in Czechoslovakia would have deep meaning for the Korbels after the war.

But in the spring of 1945, the Korbels celebrated Hitler's defeat. In July, Madlenka and her family flew back to Prague on the first plane to land in the newly free Czechoslovakia. Now eight years old, the young girl saw a city damaged, but not devastated, by the war. Most of the buildings were intact. Stones, however, had been ripped out of the streets to build barricades, and the buses and trolleys weren't running. People spent much of their time searching for food.

Young Madeleine, on the left, with her family in Prague around 1945

The Korbels were lucky; once again Josef received a prominent diplomatic assignment, as ambassador to Yugoslavia. He became the youngest member of the Czech diplomatic corps. After a brief stay in Prague, the Korbels returned to Belgrade.

The Korbels escaped the worst of the war's destruction, but the larger diplomatic and military issues raised by World War II left a lasting impression on Madeleine Albright. She saw the dangers of Britain's policy of appeasement. She understood the necessity, at times, to use force. "My mind-set is Munich," she said later, "most of my generation's is Vietnam. I saw what happened when a country was allowed to take over a piece of a country and the country went down the tubes. And I saw the opposite when America joined the fight."[8]

The war years clearly shaped Albright's ideas on how to conduct America's foreign policy. The events of the next few years—political and personal—would prove just as influential.

CHAPTER 3

"A very remarkable girl from a very remarkable family"

DENVER POST, 12/6/96

Yugoslavia, like most of Europe, had seen huge changes during and after World War II. The country now had a Communist government supported by the Soviet Union. When Josef Korbel returned to Belgrade, many of his old friends were suspicious of him, since he still favored democracy.

When Madlenka was ten, she was sent to boarding school in Switzerland. There, she learned that if she wanted to eat, she needed to speak French, and she soon mastered her third language. She also picked up a new name: Madeleine.

During vacations, Madeleine returned to Belgrade. On special occasions, she greeted her father's guests. Later, Albright recalled her duties: "You know the little girl in the national costume who gives flowers at the airport? I used to do that for a living."[1]

In Belgrade, Madeleine's father saw the realities of life under a Communist government. People who opposed the ruling regime were called enemies and traitors. They were arrested and sometimes killed. In Czechoslovakia, the Soviet Union used its military presence in most of the country to influence political affairs. For an uneasy two years, supporters of the Western allies, like Korbel, shared power with Czechoslovakia's Soviet-backed Communists. Edvard Beneš, the pro-democratic president of the country, told Korbel, "I shall defend our democracy until the last breath."[2] But by 1948, political chaos, stirred by the Communists, doomed Czech democracy.

In late 1947 the Czech Communist party had more than 1 million members, and it dominated the government. Although democrats like Beneš still served, the Communists wielded most of the real power. Beneš, perhaps fearful of a violent overthrow, had his palace guarded by soldiers from the so-called Western Brigade, Czech troops who fought with the British and Americans during the war.

Beneš's fears were justified. The president shared power with Prime Minister Klement Gottwald, a Communist. In February 1948, as a national election approached, Gottwald and his followers began to exploit their power in key agencies. On February 24 the Communists seized control of the government, shut down the free press, and ordered the army to support the Soviet Union. Police patrolled with machine guns, and supporters of democracy cried in the streets of Prague. Czech freedom was once again crushed.

The next day, a group of students marched in support of Beneš and democracy. Police fired at the marchers and beat them with rifle butts. Beneš, who was seriously ill, did not want to risk a bloody confrontation with the Communists. He accepted their control and stepped down.

In Belgrade, Josef Korbel watched with alarm as the Communists waged their revolution. He made plans with the British ambassador to once again flee with his family to England. But before he did that, Korbel returned to Czechoslovakia to attend the funeral of one of the country's last democratic leaders, Jan Masaryk, who had been murdered by being thrown from a window.

Masaryk, the foreign minister, was the son of Czechoslovakia's first president and a national hero. He and Korbel had worked side by side in London during the war and after it in Prague. It was after a conversation with Soviet leader Josef Stalin that Masaryk realized that the Soviets really controlled their country, not the Czechs. Before his death, Masaryk warned Korbel of what was to come.

Although Korbel was still a devoted democrat, he received an offer from the Communist government for a new diplomatic mission: representing Czechoslovakia on a United Nations committee. Korbel readily accepted, knowing that he could use the new post to ensure his family's safety. Korbel traveled to India as a member of the UN Commission on India and Pakistan, while his family left Central Europe for the last time.

The Korbels again traveled to England, then headed for America and settled in New York. By November 1948, Madeleine was attending sixth grade in the town of Great Neck on Long Island. Her father applied for asylum for the family—permission to remain permanently in America. Korbel wrote to U.S. officials: "I cannot, of course, return to the Communist Czechoslovakia as I would be arrested for my faithful adherence to the ideals of democracy."[3] Korbel's fears were justified. In 1949 many of his former diplomatic associates were arrested and tried as "enemies of the revolution." Some were executed. The Korbels received their asylum.

Josef Korbel finished up his work for the United Nations, and Madeleine completed the school year in Great Neck. Knowing English helped her get along (though she spoke with a British accent), and Madeleine adapted quickly to her American life. As an adult, Albright credited her social ease to her early years: "I think it has to do with the fact that I lived in a lot of countries, went to a lot of different schools, and was always being put into situations where I had to relate to people."[4] Her skill with people would prove an asset in the diplomatic world.

In 1949, Josef Korbel took a new job, as professor of international relations at the University of Denver. Madeleine and the family drove across America in a Ford coupe, and her father settled in to his new position. He started with just a one-year contract with the university, but he ended up teaching there twenty-seven years.

Unlike most professors, Korbel had seen at firsthand many of the world's recent international crises. His life experiences added more drama than any teachings from a book, though Korbel did write his own, drawing on his first-hand knowledge of European events. His first book, about communism in Yugoslavia, was published in 1951.

In Denver, Madeleine again quickly adapted to her new life. She was a dedicated student and she won a scholarship to the Kent School for Girls, a small, private high school. Like many teens, Madeleine argued with her father about school; she didn't want to attend a private school, but he insisted. Madeleine went. Secretary Albright once said that this was the only showdown she ever had with her father. Overall, she had a close relationship with Josef, and she shared his interest in international affairs and history. Madeleine wrote term papers on Eastern Europe and India and started her own international relations club, making herself president. She also won the Rocky Mountain Empire United Nations Contest, after reciting all the members of the UN in alphabetical order. Madeleine's sister Kathy remembered her older sister as "the responsible one. She was very serious."[5]

Classmates at Kent also recalled Madeleine's serious side. "She was always up to her neck in political debates and conversations," said one student. "She could hang around and talk girl talk and then turn around and debate the entire Republican school."[6] The future secretary of state was already showing her preference for Democratic party politics, but her sense of humor, one classmate said, "sometimes made the liberal medicine go down easier for some of us."[7]

By her senior year, Madeleine was president of the student council. She had lost her English accent and seemed like a typical American teen. Her dating experiences, however, were not always so typical. Her father, reflecting his "Old World" values, insisted on following Madeleine on her dates. Then he would drive his daughter home, with the boy trailing behind.

In the spring of 1955, Madeleine graduated first in a class of sixteen students. Years later, she praised the education she received at the school she had once resisted attending. But now, ready to enter college, she could step out from under her father's concerned gaze. Madeleine's hard work at Kent had earned her another scholarship, and she prepared to return to the east coast to start classes at Wellesley College, just outside Boston.

At Wellesley, she majored in political science and was active in the 1956 presidential campaign. Once again Madeleine found herself to be one of the few Democrats on a largely Republican campus. In November, she sadly watched her candidate, Adlai Stevenson, lose to President Dwight D. Eisenhower.

Madeleine's journalism career began with the school newspaper, the *Wellesley College News*. Perhaps reflecting her cosmopolitan and multilingual background, one piece she wrote was about the importance of foreign languages. She also covered visits to the area by a popular young U.S. senator from Massachusetts, John F. Kennedy. (During his 1958 reelection campaign, Kennedy stopped at Wellesley, and Madeleine reported on his speech and the enthusiastic welcome he received. "The Senator was surrounded by autograph hunters," she wrote. "Smiling, he signed a great many for them—one for me, too."[8] A little more than two years later, Kennedy was president of the United States.)

During her summer vacation in 1957, Madeleine took an intern position at her hometown newspaper, *The Denver Post*. Working in the library, she met an-

Putting together the Wellesley College News in 1958.
Madeleine is in the center.

other summer intern, Joseph Medill Patterson
Albright. Joe came from a wealthy family of newspaper publishers. He was named for his grandfather,
Joseph Medill Patterson, the founder of the *New York
Daily News.* Albright was the name of Joe's stepfather, who adopted him.

Joe had recently turned twenty and attended Williams College in Massachusetts. The two aspiring
journalists got along well. During the next few years,
they dated and fell in love. On June 11, 1959, three
days after she graduated with honors from Wellesley,

Madeleine married Joe, and the couple immediately left for Chicago. Joe had landed a job as a reporter with *The Chicago Sun-Times.*

Happily married "to the man of my dreams,"[9] Madeleine set out to find a job in journalism, too. But she soon learned that her academic honors and life experience weren't enough to secure a job in the newsrooms of Chicago.

CHAPTER 4

"I wanted to be like my father"

After settling in Chicago, Madeleine interviewed with an editor at the *Sun-Times*. He told her that union rules prevented the paper from hiring the spouse of a reporter, and the city's other papers would be reluctant to hire the wife of a reporter working for a competitor. "So, honey," the *Sun-Times* editor said, "why don't you think of another career?"[1]

Albright bristled at the editor's tone, but she didn't fight his suggestion—as she would have done years later. "As it turns out," she recalled, "it was very lucky, because I would have been a lousy reporter. . . ."[2] Instead, She found a job doing public relations for the *Encyclopaedia Britannica*. Madeleine left the company in 1961, when she and Joe moved to Long Island, where Joe had taken a job with *Newsday*.

The Long Island paper was barely twenty years old, but it had already won respect among journalists. Joe had family ties to *Newsday;* it was owned by his aunt, Alicia Patterson. Joe was the sixth generation of Pattersons to work in journalism. As he settled into his new job, Madeleine prepared to take on a new role as well, as the mother of twins. Daughters Alice and Anne were born shortly after the Albrights arrived on Long Island.

Not everything went smoothly for Madeleine and the girls. The twins were born six weeks premature and were put in incubation at first. To help take her mind off the twins' health, Madeleine started studying another language, Russian. Even after the babies were healthy, Madeleine kept up with her studies and soon became fluent.

Albright juggled her time to combine her family duties with graduate school. Still interested in politics and foreign affairs, Madeleine took courses at Columbia University's Russian Institute and the Department of Public Law and Government. She and Joe also had a third child, Katherine, in 1967. The following year, Madeleine's hard academic work paid off as she received a certificate from the Russian Institute and a master's degree from Columbia. She did her thesis on the Soviet Union's diplomatic service.

Madeleine barely had time to savor her academic accomplishment when the Albrights were on the move again. Joe was named chief of the *Newsday* bureau in Washington, D.C. The family settled in the nation's capital, but Madeleine kept some ties to New York, continuing to study at Columbia as she pursued a Ph.D.

For her doctoral thesis, Madeleine turned to her roots in Czechoslovakia. Twenty years earlier, she and the Korbels had fled Communist rule in their homeland. Since then, Czechoslovakia's politics had been

Madeleine with the twins, Alice and Anne, in 1961

dominated by the Soviet Union. In 1968, shortly after Madeleine finished her master's degree, the Czechs were trying once again to assert their independence.

A group of reformers won power in Czechoslovakia. Although still Communists, they wanted "communism with a human face," which meant more individual freedom and less Soviet control. For a few months in 1968, the Czechs regained the sense that they were an independent people with a proud heritage. This time was later called the "Prague

Spring." But the good feelings and freedom didn't last. On August 20, Soviet troops, backed by soldiers from four other Eastern European nations, invaded Czechoslovakia. Tanks again streamed through the streets of Prague. The Soviets seized the leader of the reformist government and clashed with its supporters. The Soviets explained that they had been "invited" into Czechoslovakia to crush a revolution. The Czechs vehemently denied the claim and demanded that the Soviets withdraw. Strong words, however, could not drive out more than 75,000 troops and their guns. The Soviets reestablished their control over Czechoslovakia.

Once again combining her interest in journalism and politics, Albright began researching the role of the Czech press during the Prague Spring. For eight months, the newspapers were virtually uncensored, a rarity in Communist countries, and journalists led the way in calling for reform. Albright's project ultimately took eight years to complete. During that time, she pored over daily papers and magazines from Czechoslovakia, the Soviet Union, and France. She also interviewed Czech dissidents—reformers who had opposed the Soviet Union and were sometimes jailed for their beliefs.

While working on her thesis, Albright also faced the demands of being a mother with three children. She awoke at 4:30 every morning, worked on her project, then helped Alice, Anne, and Kathy get ready for school. At night, the four Albright women often worked together, the three girls doing their homework while their mother kept going on her Ph.D.

Joe Albright was also busy during this time. After a few more years working for *Newsday*, he took a job in 1971 as a legislative assistant to Senator Edmund Muskie. A prominent Democrat from Maine, Muskie had been his party's candidate for vice president in 1968, and he ran for the Democratic presidential nomination in the 1972 election. Joe's ties to Muskie gave Madeleine her first direct link to politics since her years at Wellesley.

Among her friends in Washington, Madeleine was known as an effective fund-raiser. She served on the board of directors of the Beauvoir School, the private school that Alice and Anne attended, and led a successful fund-raising drive. In 1972 she put her persuasive personality to work for Senator Muskie, helping him raise money for his presidential campaign. One dinner she organized raised $175,000 for the candidate, his most successful fund-raiser of the race.

Muskie's campaign, however, was a short one; in April he withdrew from the race. Muskie had failed to appeal to most Democratic voters. He was also plagued by Republican "dirty tricks." President Richard Nixon's aides orchestrated an effort to use their supporters as spies on Muskie's staff and tried to disrupt his fund-raisers.

Even after Muskie quit the race, Albright and some other volunteers refused to give up, continuing to make phone solicitations. Muskie appreciated this loyalty. He remained an influential Democrat and a friend of the Albrights, and he later give Madeleine a further boost in Washington circles.

Despite the setback for Muskie, 1972 was a big year for the Albrights. Joe published a book, *What Makes Spiro Run?*, a study of Vice President Spiro Agnew. Joe also left his job with Muskie and became the Washington correspondent for the *San Francisco Chronicle*. Madeleine, meanwhile, continued working on her thesis.

In 1975, Joe had another job change, taking a position with a national newspaper chain. The next year, Madeleine's long years of hard work finally paid off. She received her Ph.D., and Columbia University Press published her dissertation, *The Role of the Press in Political Change: Czechoslovakia, 1968*. Like her father, she could now use her academic success and passion for world events to educate others.

But before Albright ever stepped into a classroom, Senator Ed Muskie came to her with an exciting offer. She was about to enter a working environment far different from the Chicago newsroom she had walked into fifteen years before, looking for her first job.

In 1976, another national election year, Ed Muskie again considered running for president. He named Madeleine Albright the Washington coordinator of "Maine for Muskie," an organization that explored the senator's chances for securing the presidential nomination. In the end, Muskie decided that his chances weren't good, and he did not enter the race.

Muskie, however, still had his seat in the Senate, and he needed a chief legislative assistant to help him with his duties. Instead of choosing someone who had worked on Capitol Hill before, Muskie picked Madeleine Albright.

Although she had never held a paid political job, Madeleine did have her Ph.D. and a tenacious commitment to any task she undertook. Her academic background was a plus: The Ph.D. ". . . made it possible for Senator Muskie to introduce me as Dr. Albright, instead of Madeleine Albright, little housewife."[3]

Through the end of the 1976 congressional session, Muskie was on the Senate Foreign Relations Committee, so Albright's expertise on Eastern Europe and the Soviet Union was a valuable resource. When the new session started in January 1977, Muskie was named chairman of the Senate Budget Committee, which helps to decide which government projects will be funded and how much money they get. Muskie was now one of the most important lawmakers in Washington.

Albright worked behind the scenes for Muskie, coordinating research and, on the Senate floor, helping him pass legislation. Along the way she learned about the art of compromise, the lubricant that makes politics—and diplomacy—flow. Albright's political skills would prove useful later in her career.

Albright also found time to help her father, Josef Korbel. Over the years, Korbel's prominence at the University of Denver and in academic circles had grown as he continued to publish scholarly works. At Denver, he helped create the Graduate School of International Studies and directed the school's Social Studies Foundation.

In 1977, at sixty-nine, Korbel was still teaching, still exploring the history of his beloved homeland. He wrote his last book, *20th Century Czechoslovakia:*

The Meanings of Its History, and asked his daughter, now a scholar of Eastern European affairs herself, to review the manuscript before it was published. Madeleine would never have another chance to work so closely with her father. On July 18, 1977, Korbel died of pancreatic cancer in a Denver hospital. Madeleine not only lost her father, whom she loved so much, but also the man who inspired her to work so hard at everything she did and who stirred her interest in politics, journalism, and academics. Madeleine's brother, John, appreciated that she had a "special relationship" with their father, "partly because she followed so closely in his footsteps."[4]

After Korbel's death, his colleagues published a book about Czechoslovakian history in his honor. One essay summed up Korbel's life and his philosophy: "Above all else, Josef Korbel loved freedom, and the ennobling dignity of the individual that it alone can nourish."[5]

Korbel had shared that love of freedom with his daughter, along with a dedication to public service. In her next job, Albright again used her academic expertise to serve the government. In March 1978 she left her position with Senator Muskie and began working for one of her former professors at Columbia, Zbigniew Brzezinski.

Brzezinski, born in Poland, ran Columbia's Institute on Communist Affairs. In the 1960s he was often quoted in the press for his expert views on U.S. relations with the Soviet Union and Eastern Europe. The professor and Albright had many things in common.

Brzezinski's father had also been a diplomat. After World War II, the Brzezinskis left Poland when the Communists took over. In America, Brzezinski became a well-known scholar and author on Eastern Europe. And in an interesting coincidence, he married a relative of Edvard Beneš, the president of Czechoslovakia when Josef Korbel held his last diplomatic position in his homeland.

After the election of 1976, President Jimmy Carter named Brzezinski head of the National Security Council (NSC). The NSC had been created after World War II, at the beginning of the Cold War with the Soviet Union. The NSC gave American presidents another viewpoint on foreign affairs and defense issues, along with those of the State Department and the military.

Brzezinski, as Carter's national security adviser, was considered fairly conservative. He had supported the war in Vietnam, saw a need to sometimes talk tough with the Soviets, and gave the impression he wouldn't make any dramatic policy changes. "U.S. foreign policy is like an aircraft carrier," he said. "You simply don't send it into a 180-degree turn; at most you move it a few degrees to port or starboard."[6]

As one of the "crew" on this aircraft carrier, Madeleine Albright was assigned to help Brzezinski and the NSC work with Congress. Her title was Congressional Relations Officer, and her time with Senator Muskie gave her insight into how legislators think and act. Brzezinski was grateful for her expertise. "She kept me from getting into trouble with Congress," he said.[7]

Albright had an office in the White House, and her main focus was foreign-policy legislation. In her role, Brzezinski said, "Albright not only became a key

NSC staffer, but greatly reinforced the occasionally sputtering overall White House coordination with Congress."[8]

During Albright's three years on the NSC, the United States faced a number of crucial foreign-policy issues. President Carter signed a treaty promising to give control of the Panama Canal to Panama in 1999. The treaty was highly controversial; some people worried what would happen to U.S. commercial shipping and naval forces if the canal ever fell into hostile hands. Some Republicans thought the treaty was a sign of President Carter's weakness in foreign affairs.

Carter won praise, however, for arranging a peace treaty between Israel and Egypt. For two weeks at Camp David, the presidential Maryland retreat, Carter mediated between Israel's Menachem Begin and Egypt's Anwar Sadat. The treaty ended a state of war between the two nations that had existed for thirty years.

In the Cold War struggle with the Soviet Union, Carter ordered a grain embargo when the Soviets invaded Afghanistan at the end of 1979. And in the largest foreign-policy crisis of the era, America watched helplessly as Muslim radicals took fifty-six Americans hostage at the U.S. embassy in Tehran, Iran.

Albright and the other NSC staffers had to deal with these complex issues while working for a boss who could be difficult. Many Washington insiders considered Brzezinski arrogant and ambitious, hoping one day to become secretary of state. Carter's secretary of state, Cyrus Vance, didn't like Brzezinski. Relations between the State Department and the Na-

President Jimmy Carter shakes hands with Senator Edmund Muskie after announcing that he would nominate Muskie to be his secretary of state. Between Muskie and Carter is Zbigniew Brzezinski, national security adviser.

tional Security Council didn't improve much when Vance was replaced by Albright's old boss, Edmund Muskie. But whatever happened around her, Albright took the same approach to her work: ". . . use the knowledge that I had, work hard and have a good time—my version of a good time . . . which is to work hard."[9]

In 1980 the Iranian hostage crisis, along with a struggling economy, crushed President Carter's chances for reelection, and in early 1981, Albright was out of a job. She took a position at the Center for Strategic and International Studies, a research center based in Washington, where she served as a fellow in Soviet and Eastern European affairs. Albright studied developments in the Soviet Union and its allies.

Albright also won a fellowship at the Smithsonian Institute's Woodrow Wilson Center for Scholars. During her year at the Wilson Center, Albright wrote her second book, *Poland: The Role of the Press and Political Change.*

Albright, who speaks and reads Polish, traveled to Poland to conduct interviews for her book, which was similar to her Ph.D. dissertation on Czechoslovakia in 1968. She examined the influence of the media during the rise of Solidarity, the Polish labor movement led by Lech Walesa. Walesa and Solidarity fought Poland's Communist leaders for greater freedom and won—for a time. In December 1981 the government clamped down on the media and instituted tighter control on all of Polish society.

Brzezinski wrote an introduction for the book. He called her efforts "academically solid and politically incisive."[10] Edmund Muskie also endorsed the work, saying that Albright's insights were "an invaluable contribution to our understanding of a period that captured the world's spotlight."[11]

With her book, Albright continued amassing credentials that made her an expert in Soviet and Eastern European affairs. In 1982 she was ready to begin another phase of her professional development, as a college professor. But 1982 also brought the greatest personal challenge that Albright had faced since coming to America.

CHAPTER 5

"Women have to interrupt"

WASHINGTON POST, 1/6/97

While Madeleine Albright was finishing her Ph.D. and entering the world of national politics, her husband Joe continued his successful journalism career. In 1976 he became a Washington correspondent for the Cox newspaper chain. Three years later, his peers recognized his talents by giving him an award for distinguished reporting on political events in the nation's capital. But by the beginning of 1982, Joe faced a turning point in his life that would impact his whole family.

On January 13, 1982, a heavy snow blanketed Georgetown, the fashionable part of Washington where the Albrights lived. That morning, in the family's living room, Joe sat across from his wife and said, "This marriage is dead and I'm in love with somebody else."[1]

Madeleine was stunned. After almost twenty-three years together, she thought she and Joe had a happy, thriving marriage, with a beautiful family.

Twin daughters Alice and Anne had gone to college and majored in history, just like their father. Kate was an equally promising high-school student. But for once, Madeleine's tenacity could not change the outcome of the situation.

"I did not want a divorce," Albright later said. "But life goes on."[2] After Joe left and the divorce went through, Madeleine received the family's Georgetown house and a 370-acre (150-hectare) farm in Virginia. Financially, she and her daughters were secure. But emotionally, Madeleine took a long time to heal from the split, and she has never seriously dated again. Over time, however, the divorce proved beneficial in some ways: "I think it made me more self-reliant. . . . I think if it taught me anything, it was to rely on my own judgment and to do what I need to do for my daughters and myself."[3]

Albright shared some of those lessons as she began her teaching career at Georgetown University, a Catholic school in Washington well known for its academic rigor. The university hired Albright in 1982 to teach international affairs at its School of Foreign Service.

Albright wanted young women to have the chance to meet professionals in the foreign-service community, explore job opportunities, and discuss international trends and events, so she instituted the Women in Foreign Service Program, an extracurricular program for graduate students. Throughout her time at Georgetown, Albright was committed to sharing with her female students what she had learned in the male-dominated worlds of politics and academia. Women who did succeed, she believed, had a special obligation to help other women. The Women in Foreign Service Program was one way of extending that helping hand.

In the classroom at Georgetown, Albright focused on her specialty, the politics of Eastern and Central Europe, as well as U.S. foreign policy. She had a way of presenting complex issues in a straightforward, engaging way. She was popular with the students, who four times voted her Georgetown's teacher of the year. Some of her colleagues, however, did not consider her a deep scholar, despite her past accomplishments. "I never thought of myself—or I was never allowed to think of myself—as a serious academic," Albright said after her years at Georgetown. "I came into academia late. I'm not one of those people who wrote great tomes."[4]

Outside of the classroom, Albright was still involved in Democratic politics. She began holding a series of dinners at her home for Democratic Party leaders and advisers. These dinners were sometimes compared to the eighteenth-century salons of Europe, in which aristocrats and intellectuals gathered to discuss art, literature, and current affairs. Albright's dinners, though, focused on foreign policy.

At a typical Albright gathering, she would introduce a particular topic, then ask the guests questions to start a general discussion. Albright called the evenings ". . . working dinners, where people can surface their ideas to see what their validity is. People don't feel it's a confrontational setting; they feel it is a comfortable setting."[5]

With those dinners, Albright added to her status as a major Democratic expert on foreign affairs. In

1984 her reputation among party leaders led Walter Mondale to tap Albright as a foreign-policy adviser during his presidential campaign.

Mondale, former vice president under Jimmy Carter, faced a tough race. President Ronald Reagan was running for reelection, and his upbeat personality and conservative views were popular with most voters—even many Democrats. Mondale was a traditional liberal Democrat, supportive of civil rights, the environment, and labor groups. In foreign policy, he favored a less confrontational stance with the Soviet Union than the one Reagan championed.

Albright, although she shared most of Mondale's liberal views, tended to be a little tougher toward the Soviets than most Democrats, probably a result of her family's experience. Despite this philosophical difference, Albright was a valued part of the Mondale team, and she spent much of her time advising Mondale's choice for vice president, Geraldine Ferraro. A congresswoman from New York, Ferraro was the first woman ever nominated as a vice-presidential candidate by a major party.

In July, Mondale, Ferraro, and the campaign's top advisers met at Lake Tahoe, in California, to discuss their strategy. Albright was there, and she later accompanied Ferraro back to the candidate's home in the borough of Queens, New York City.

In the House of Representatives, Ferraro focused mostly on domestic issues, so Albright helped sharpen her knowledge of foreign affairs. Albright gave her reports on arms control and various countries, and Ferraro taped all their conversations. "I listened to [those] tapes wherever I went," Ferraro said.

"I played them back in the car, in the kitchen, even in the bathtub at night."[6]

Whenever Ferraro dealt with foreign policy, Albright was there. She sat in on a meeting between Ferraro and Robert McFarlane, President Reagan's national security adviser. At the meeting, McFarlane briefed the candidate on the nation's top-secret security issues. In October, Albright spent hours at a time helping Ferraro prepare for her debate with Vice President George Bush.

Mondale and other Democrats had hoped that Ferraro would help the party take advantage of the "gender gap"; in most polls, women opposed President Reagan's policies much more than men did. Albright also accepted the notion of the gender gap. But Ferraro's nomination showed the problems women still faced as they moved up the political ladder.

While preparing for the vice-presidential debate, even Ferraro's own staff tended to give more weight to what male advisers said. On the issue of whether Ferraro, as president, could ever launch a nuclear attack, Albright drafted an appropriate response. Then a male staffer broke in to say how he thought Ferraro should answer that question. "He sounded authoritative," Ferraro later wrote. "It seemed he was more believable than Madeleine, simply because he was a man. Maddening as this bias was, it was there."[7]

The gender gap and the historic selection of a female vice-presidential candidate didn't help the Democrats in 1984. Reagan won in a landslide, and Albright, instead of earning a job in a new Democratic administration, returned to her academic duties.

Back at Georgetown, Albright took the opportunity to blast the media's coverage of Ferraro during the campaign. Ted Koppel, of ABC's *Nightline*, came to speak at the university. Albright was sitting in the front row and commented on an interview he had done with Ferraro.

"You did a number on her," Albright called out to Koppel.

"Well, I have been accused of being professorial, prosecutorial, and pompous during that interview," Koppel replied.

"All of the above," Albright shot back in her no-nonsense way. "Which leads me to the following question: Do you believe that you, as well as other commentators, were harder on Mrs. Ferraro on foreign policy because she was a woman than you might have been on a man?"[8]

Koppel had to admit it was true.

Besides her work with Geraldine Ferraro, Albright took on another new role in 1984, as vice chairwoman of the National Democratic Institute for International Affairs. The nonpartisan institute tried to strengthen democracy in countries around the world. The next year, Albright joined the Center for National Policy, a nonprofit group allied with the Democratic party. A think tank founded in 1981, the center brought together representatives from business, labor, government, and academia to research domestic and international policy issues. Her duties with these new organizations, along with her classes at Georgetown and her family, satisfied Albright's desire to keep busy and push herself to excel.

In 1987, Albright once again took a break from the classroom to work behind the scenes on a presidential campaign. One of the Democratic party candidates for the next year's election was Michael Dukakis, the governor of Massachusetts. During her time with Walter Mondale in 1984, Albright had met John Sasso and Susan Estrich, two Democratic advisers. In the 1988 campaign, they worked for Governor Dukakis, and Sasso asked Albright if she would like to work for the governor. Albright readily agreed, taking the position without pay.

In this campaign, Albright was her candidate's major foreign-policy adviser. She relied on her contacts in academia and Washington's circle of experts to give Dukakis ". . . access to as many people from as wide a spectrum as possible on the foreign policy issues. . . . The most important thing is not that he has my views but that he has information and I serve as the honest broker and a good conduit to make sure he has what he needs."[9]

Although she saw herself as a collector of resources, Albright played a key role in writing speeches for Dukakis and hammering out his positions on foreign affairs. That prominent role brought Albright her first national attention, as major newspapers such as *The New York Times* and *The Christian Science Monitor* interviewed her to learn Dukakis's stance on issues and to find out who she was. Rumors circulated that she was a likely candidate for national security adviser. But before she could think about a future government job, Albright had to help elect Michael Dukakis.

In July 1988, Dukakis won the Democratic party's presidential nomination. His opponent was Vice

President George Bush, who shared many of President Reagan's conservative views and inherited much of his support among voters. Albright wanted to show Americans that in foreign affairs, the Reagan-Bush team had often failed to do what was best for the country. A prime example was the Iran-contra affair.

In a complex, secret deal, the Reagan administration had sold military weapons to Iran, in exchange for the release of American hostages held by terrorist groups supported by Iran. U.S.-Iranian relations had been strained since 1979, when Iran's fundamentalist Islamic government had taken another group of Americans hostage. American public opinion remained hostile to Iran, and President Reagan had talked tough about never dealing with the Iranians to win the release of the current hostages.

When news of the secret arms-for-hostages negotiation first appeared in 1986, many Americans were shocked. Adding to the outrage among some people, especially Democrats, was the second part of the affair: The money made from the arms deals was used to fund anti-Communist Nicaraguan rebels. Congress had passed a law prohibiting the Reagan administration from helping these "contras."

The whole affair was called the Iran-contra scandal; some journalists nicknamed it "Contragate," a reference to the Watergate scandal under President Richard Nixon a decade before. Whatever it was called, to Albright the shady dealings were a disastrous foreign policy—and a prime campaign issue for Governor Dukakis to exploit. "We will use it as an example of secretive policy or diplomacy and lack of judgment," Albright said. "It was a lousy policy that led us into the Persian Gulf. You cannot make policy by such a hare-brained way of getting around the bureaucracy."[10]

In contrast to the Republicans, Albright said, Dukakis would consult regularly with Congress before making major foreign-policy decisions. "[Dukakis] knows you cannot have an effective foreign policy without Congress."[11]

Albright had one of her first chances to help shape Dukakis's foreign-policy image even before he officially won the Democratic nomination, on another issue involving Iran. On July 3, 1988, a U.S. naval ship, the *Vincennes*, accidentally shot down an Iranian commercial airliner over the Persian Gulf.

With no time to consult her circle of experts, Albright helped Dukakis draft his response to the event. While he regretted the accident, the governor felt the United States should have done more to end the war raging between Iran and Iraq. That conflict, and the need to protect American oil supplies, had brought U.S. ships into the Persian Gulf in the first place.

As the election campaign went on, Albright's goal was to assure voters that Dukakis had a logical, workable foreign policy. Dukakis, meanwhile, tried to demonstrate that Vice President Bush, as a top member of the Reagan administration, had helped shape a foreign policy that threatened American interests around the world. Bush, said Dukakis, "doesn't have what it takes to lead this country when it comes to foreign policy."[12]

In one of her major areas of expertise, the Soviet Union, Albright again helped distinguish Dukakis from George Bush and the Republicans. During the Reagan-Bush years, America tried to intimidate the Soviets by increasing its arsenal of nuclear weapons and introducing the idea of a space-based antimissile system, nicknamed "Star Wars." Albright and Dukakis believed that America had to strengthen its nonnuclear military force—without wasting billions of dollars, as they accused Reagan of doing in his spending for conventional weapons.

The Soviets had begun to change during the mid-1980s. Mikhail Gorbachev, who came to power in 1985, seemed willing to discuss arms reductions with the United States, for both nuclear and conventional weapons. And Gorbachev loosened some of the restraints on his own citizens, introducing "glasnost," a policy of greater domestic freedom. These changes intrigued Albright, but she said that Dukakis, if elected president, would challenge exactly how much Gorbachev meant what he said.

Still slightly more of "hawk" than many Democrats, Albright saw a need for America to keep up its guard against its longtime foe, while welcoming any real changes that occurred there. What she didn't know was how soon major changes would come to the Soviet Union and all of Eastern Europe, ending America's traditional post–World War II foreign policy.

When those changes came, however, Albright couldn't play a part in shaping America's response to them. Once again, her candidate did not win. On November 8, 1988, Vice President Bush easily beat Michael Dukakis for the presidency. Albright returned to Washington and her think tanks and the life of a professor.

In 1989, Albright became president of the Center for National Policy. She also did a favor that year for a new friend, the young governor from Arkansas, Bill Clinton. Albright had met him in 1988, when Clinton came to Boston to help with the Dukakis campaign. Clinton also gave the nominating speech for Dukakis at the Democratic convention.

Clinton and Albright's backgrounds were different: He was the product of a small town in the South, while she had grown up in a sophisticated world of diplomacy and academia. But they shared a love of politics, and they stayed in touch after the campaign.

When Clinton needed a recommendation to serve on the Council on Foreign Relations, Albright wrote one for him. She praised his intelligence and political experience. Clinton was named to the council, a nonpartisan group that discusses foreign affairs (Albright's father had once belonged to the council as well). The friendship between Clinton and Albright would continue to grow in the years to come, and Clinton eventually attended a few of Albright's famous Georgetown dinners.

In the midst of her hectic life during 1989, Albright suffered a personal loss with the death of her mother, Mandula. With both of her parents gone, Albright's ties to Czechoslovakia were fading. What she didn't know, however, was that dramatic events were about to take place in Czechoslovakia, and they would eventually bring Albright back to her homeland and into world affairs.

CHAPTER 6

"You are the land of my birth"

7/14/97 PRESS STATEMENT

Twenty years had passed since the "Prague Spring" of 1968. After the Soviet Union sent in troops that year to end Czechoslovakia's short burst of freedom, Albright's homeland returned to strict Communist control. When the ruling Communists suspected citizens of opposing the government, their mail was intercepted and read, their phones tapped, their houses searched. In many cases, people were arrested and jailed for no legal reason.

In that climate of oppression, some Czech dissidents tried to fight back, but with words, not guns. The country's most famous dissident organization was Charter 77, and its most prominent member was playwright Vaclav Havel.

Havel had spent four years in prison for writing essays attacking the Czech regime and for his human-rights activities with Charter 77. When he was released in 1983, he continued to speak out against Czechoslovakia's Communist rulers. But by 1988 something changed in Czechoslovakia and across Eastern Europe.

The Soviet Union, under Mikhail Gorbachev, was no longer hostile to all reforms in its "satellite" nations. To some degree, each country could decide on its own how much political change to allow. Czechoslovakia's Communist leaders did not welcome Gorbachev's policy, but the Czech people did. This new freedom led to public demonstrations against the country's Communist party.

The first major rally took place on August 21, 1988, to mark the 20th anniversary of the Soviet invasion. Some 10,000 people marched and shouted anti-Soviet slogans. For the next year, the demonstrations grew, both here and throughout Eastern Europe, until hundreds of thousands of Czechs peacefully gathered in the streets of Prague. The Communist leaders tried to suppress the rallies, but many police officers and army leaders supported the demonstrations. In November 1989 the Czech Communist party realized it had lost control of the country.

Vaclav Havel was a key leader of the antigovernment marchers, and when a new government was formed in December, Havel was named president of Czechoslovakia. The protesters had created what some people called the "Velvet Revolution"—a nonviolent dismantling of the old communist system.

In his first important address to the newly free land, Havel touched on the past dictatorship and the struggles ahead for the Czechs. He called on the citizens to "teach ourselves and others that politics should be an expression of a desire to contribute to the happiness of the community rather than of a need

Hundreds of thousands of people packed the street to Wenceslas Square on November 21, 1989. It was the largest protest rally in Czechoslovakia in memory. The banner in the middle of this photograph says "free elections."

to cheat or rape the community."[1] Finally, Havel closed with this stirring guarantee: "People, your government has returned to you!"[2]

Albright closely followed the events in her homeland, and she grew excited when one day she heard a familiar name mentioned in a news report. Jiri Dienstbier had been named foreign minister in Havel's new government. More than two decades before, Dienstbier and Albright had become friends when she interviewed him for research on her dissertation. Dienstbier had been a news correspondent for Czech radio in 1968, and he gave Albright valuable insights into the role of the media during those heady days of the Prague Spring. Dienstbier returned to Czechoslovakia in 1969. He eventually became a spokesman for Charter 77 and, like Havel, served time in jail for his dissident activities. Also like Havel, Dienstbier was one of the leading figures during the Velvet Revolution. In December 1989, when the Communists were defeated, he helped cut the barbed-wire fence that sealed Czechoslovakia from Western Europe, a symbolic gesture of the country's new freedom.

Now, Dienstbier was one of Havel's top cabinet members, and Albright immediately called her old friend. Dienstbier said he would arrange a meeting between Havel and Albright, and she returned to Czechoslovakia for the first time in more than forty years.

During her meeting with Havel, Albright learned that the president was going to visit the United States in February 1990. Albright offered to help Havel and his staff when he came to Washington. Then, her visit over, she returned home.

"All of a sudden," Albright later recounted, "I get this phone call saying yes indeed they would love to have some help."[3] Albright's home quickly turned into the headquarters for President Havel's advance people, who worked out the details of his trip to America, while student volunteers manned the phone and fax machine.

When Havel arrived in Washington on February 20, Albright met him at the Czechoslovakian embassy. She went over the president's schedule and advised him about the American leaders he would meet when he addressed a joint session of Congress. The speech went well, with Havel winning five standing ovations. Speaking in Czech, he said how strange it was for him, a writer with no political background, to be addressing such a powerful legislative body. "I have not attended any school for presidents," Havel said. "My only school was life itself."[4]

Americans were captivated by the humble writer's rise to lead one of the world's newest democracies, and Albright was a trusted aide during his trip.

After his successful speech, Havel went to New York. He had visited the city years before, and he reacquainted himself with old friends. Albright was there, too, and she went to a party given in Havel's honor, serving as his interpreter. The room was filled with famous American writers, including playwrights Arthur Miller and Edward Albee and author Norman Mailer. Albright translated the words of these literary dignitaries into Czech for Havel and thought to herself, "I do not believe this."[5]

Albright's friendship with Havel continued to deepen. In May 1990, she returned to Prague and stayed at the president's home. In August, Albright accompanied Havel and his wife to Bermuda for a vacation. She reminisced: ". . . we talked about American politics, and we talked about Eastern European politics, and we talked about Gorbachev. It was two days of solid talking."[6]

Havel and Albright shared a common language and cultural heritage, but with Albright the Czech president also had a seasoned adviser who could offer insights into his country's affairs from a knowledgeable American perspective. American support—moral and financial—would be crucial for Czechoslovakia to overcome its Communist past. With Albright as a friend, Havel had a sympathetic ear in Washington, though neither of them knew at the time how influential Albright would ultimately become.

But their relationship wasn't all business. On an October trip back to the United States, the two, along with some other acquaintances, walked through New York's Times Square. Like a typical tourist, Havel bought an "I Love New York" T-shirt, and Albright took the group to a popular site for visiting writers, the Algonguin Hotel. In the 1920s and 1930s, some of America's best writers gathered there for drinks and witty conversation. Now, Albright toasted her famous writer friend in the same lounge.

Aside from her pleasurable trips to Czechoslovakia, Albright also had plenty of work to do that year. In August 1990, Iraq, led by Saddam Hussein, invaded Kuwait, one of America's allies bordering the Persian Gulf. Because of the region's huge oil reserves, the Middle East has been a major concern for American leaders for decades. The prime issue is making sure that oil keeps flowing out of the Middle Eastern ground and into American fuel tanks. Iraq's invasion of Kuwait was a serious threat to that safe flow of oil, since Saddam would have most likely gone after another target next: Saudi Arabia, owner of the world's largest oil reserves.

By October, President George Bush was thinking of sending soldiers to Kuwait to drive out the invading Iraqis. The mood in the United States was split: Some people approved of using military troops; others wanted to force Iraq to leave by imposing sanctions that would cripple the Iraqi economy.

In Congress, House Democrats turned to Albright for her opinion. She was a familiar figure on Capitol Hill, offering her expertise on a number of foreign-policy issues. She told the Democrats the United States had three choices: fight, sit tight, or negotiate. If the country chose to fight, she recommended using multinational forces, not the United States alone. But in this instance she was opposed to war; she imagined Saddam "setting off chemicals before we finish him."[7] Albright's preference was to use sanctions against Iraq.

By arguing against a war in the Middle East, Albright seemed to be taking the traditional liberal Democratic stance—something she usually didn't do when it came to events in the Soviet Union or Eastern Europe. Her recommendation bothered one of the other experts who met with Congress that day, Professor Barry Rubin. "Albright was acting in a foolishly partisan manner, warning them that Bush might do something sneaky, which he did not. She was playing to the worst instincts of the Democrats."[8]

In the end, most Democrats supported Bush's plan to send troops to the Middle East. American forces, helped by soldiers from dozens of other nations, drove

Saddam's forces out of Kuwait. Albright later admitted she had been wrong to counsel against using force. But the Persian Gulf War did implement an action she approved of: using a multinational military force—not just U.S. troops—to combat aggressors. Albright's stance on Iraq in 1990 didn't diminish her influence within the Democratic party. Even before the 1992 election, some Democratic leaders, including old friend Ed Muskie, hinted that if the Democrats took back the White House, Albright was in line for a top foreign-policy position. But first, the Democrats had to win the election.

CHAPTER 7

"I would like to help elect a Democratic President"

WASHINGTON POST, 1/6/91

After America's swift victory in the Persian Gulf War, President George Bush seemed on his way to reelection in 1992. Successful military operations tend to boost a president's popularity, and Bush's favorable rating among voters soared. The Democrats didn't offer any candidates who could match Bush's experience, especially in foreign affairs.

Despite the long odds, seven Democrats declared themselves candidates for their party's presidential nomination. Arkansas governor Bill Clinton launched his campaign on October 3, 1991, hoping to fulfill the final part of a dream that began back in high school. In 1963 a teenage Clinton visited the White House and shook hands with his political idol, President John F. Kennedy. That moment cemented Clinton's ambition to enter politics and perhaps someday run for president himself.

Early in the campaign, Clinton faced accusations about his personal life and his avoidance of military service during the Vietnam War. Clinton appeared on TV to respond to some of the charges, and he vowed to carry on with his campaign in New Hampshire, the site of the first Democratic primary. Clinton overcame the bad publicity and finished second in New Hampshire. An energized Clinton called himself "the Comeback Kid." In the months ahead he continued to deal with the questions about his character and convinced many Democrats he would be an effective leader.

Madeleine Albright, as president of the Center for National Policy, was officially neutral during the early part of the campaign. Working for a think tank with broad Democratic connections, she couldn't appear to favor one Democrat over another. But after meeting with Clinton in the spring of 1992, her sympathies were clearly with the young governor she had befriended four years before. Once Clinton won the Democratic presidential nomination in July 1992, Albright brought her knowledge to the Clinton camp, helping the candidate shape his views on foreign-policy issues.

Foreign policy, however, was not the key issue in 1992. Unless the country is at war or close to entering one, foreign policy rarely plays a large part in a U.S. presidential campaign. Clinton and his advisers adopted as their unofficial slogan "It's the economy, stupid." Clinton constantly stressed that President Bush had ignored the economic needs of the working and middle classes. Bush tried to convince voters that his many years of public service made him the best-qualified candidate. And Ross Perot, a Texas billionaire who bankrolled his own party, said both of the major parties were ignoring America's real crisis, the huge federal deficit and the economy in general.

On Election Day, November 3, Clinton showed he truly was the Comeback Kid, easily beating Bush and Perot. For the first time, going back to her college days and the 1956 Adlai Stevenson campaign, Albright had backed a Democratic winner for the presidency. Now her party loyalty, academic background, and political skills made Albright an important member of the new president's team.

During the transition from the Bush to the Clinton administration, Albright was one of Clinton's top foreign-policy aides. She had an office in the White House not far from the one she used while serving on the National Security Council during the Carter administration. But Albright's role in the Clinton White House was going to be even more important than her first job in the executive branch.

In December, Albright was preparing for a party in Washington when she received a call from the Clinton staff, asking her to fly to Arkansas to discuss taking on the role of U.S. ambassador to the United Nations. Albright reportedly was not Clinton's first choice for the job, but she readily accepted the president-elect's offer. On December 22, Clinton announced that Albright was officially part of his new administration.

At a news conference that day, Albright touched on her background as an immigrant and the task that lay ahead of her: "As a result of the generous spirit of the American people, our family had the privilege of growing up as free Americans. You can therefore understand how proud I will be to sit at the United Nations behind the nameplate that says 'United States of America.'"[1]

As ambassador to the UN, Albright would be responsible for representing America's foreign-policy interests in that international body. The UN was formed after World War II to try to keep peace around the world and address global health, social, and economic problems.

The United States has extraordinary power at the UN. It is one of five permanent members on the Security Council, a fifteen-member group chiefly responsible for maintaining international peace and security. As a permanent member, the United States can veto any resolution proposed in the Security Council.

Albright was not the first American woman named UN ambassador. Jeanne Kirkpatrick, another foreign-policy expert who once taught at Georgetown University, held the post during the 1980s under President Reagan. But President-elect Clinton planned to give Albright a position of influence that few—if any—previous U.S. ambassadors had. Albright was to be an official cabinet member and sit on the National Security Council. Clinton wanted her to help shape American foreign policy, not merely voice the country's views at the UN.

Clinton's choice of Albright won a favorable reaction in Washington. Robert E. Hunter, a foreign-policy expert at the Center for Strategic and International Studies, said Albright had ". . . the capacity to sit through tedious meetings, to broker differences, to listen to people, to find common ground. In other words, when you're dealing with 160 different countries, it's the people skills that matter most, and she has them."[2]

Mary McGrory, a prominent political columnist for *The Washington Post*, also welcomed Albright's selection. McGrory applauded her intellect and her sensitivity. "She is precisely the kind of woman everyone wished could have been in the room when the men were making their disastrous decisions about Vietnam."[3]

Before assuming her new job, Albright had to face the scrutiny of the Senate Foreign Relations Committee. Most major presidential appointees must be confirmed by the Senate. The Foreign Relations Committee had the task of interviewing Albright and then making a recommendation on her capabilities to the full Senate.

On January 21, 1993, the ambassador-designate faced the men who would decide her fate. The response to her nomination was positive, but some committee members and other politicians had grown disenchanted with the United Nations and its mission.

The critics didn't like the idea of the United States being part of any international body that seemed to function like a world government, fearing America lost some of its independence. Others felt the United Nations was poorly managed and cost the United States too much money. In protest, Congress had voted to withhold its contribution to the UN. Albright not only had to sell herself to the committee; she had to promote the UN as well.

Albright began by describing her background, including her family's struggles in Communist Czechoslovakia, her father's work for the UN, and her ties to Edmund Muskie. She then stressed how important the UN was during such a crucial time in history, with the collapse of communism in Europe and the need for peacekeeping missions around world. Albright acknowledged that the UN had administrative problems, but that Congress should not turn its back on the organization just when it was poised to make a real impact on world peace.

In her conclusion, Albright focused on the work that waited for her: "The power that we have had as a nation comes from our ability to look into the future and to be on the side of change. We need to harness this power today for our work at the United Nations. I am very aware of the enormous challenges that lie ahead."[4]

After delivering her prepared remarks, Albright took questions from the committee on her views. She told the senators that the highest priority for the UN Security Council was the fighting in Bosnia, a country that was once part of Yugoslavia. Given her personal and academic background, the situation there was also one of Albright's main concerns.

The hearing ended without any controversy, and on January 27 the Senate voted unanimously to confirm Albright as the 21st U.S. Permanent Representative to the United Nations, the official title for the position. In that role, Albright followed such distinguished American politicians as Adlai Stevenson, New York Senator Daniel P. Moynihan, and President George Bush.

Albright started her job on February 1, as Secretary of State Warren Christopher introduced her to the United Nations as America's new representative.

Newly appointed as United Nations ambassador, Madeleine Albright waits while Secretary of State Warren Christopher speaks with reporters in front of the home of UN secretary-general Boutros Boutros-Ghali.

Christopher and Albright had worked in the same administration once before; he was deputy secretary of state under President Carter when Albright worked for the National Security Council. He and Albright would now work closely to shape President Clinton's foreign policy.

At the UN, Albright was one of just eight women among the more than 180 representatives there. As the American ambassador, she was clearly the most influential woman, if not the single most important ambassador. To help her with her duties, Albright inherited a staff of more than 100 people. Her apartment, a suite at the top of New York's Waldorf Towers, cost $27,000 a month, and it doubled as a guest hall where she could host visiting dignitaries. Building personal relations with other ambassadors is crucial for a successful diplomat, and the years of hosting her Georgetown salon had given Albright valuable experience at discussing complex matters over relaxed dinners.

As Albright settled into her new position, she soon learned how many difficult issues waited for her at the United Nations. Despite the end of the Cold War, the world in 1993 was filled with conflicts that America wanted to end. Albright's new responsibilities would far outweigh what she had faced as a campaign adviser or popular university professor.

The United Nations gives the world's countries a forum for discussing important issues, but when talk alone can't solve a problem, the UN can take action. Since its first peacekeeping mission in 1956, the UN has sent its military forces, composed of soldiers from the member nations, to enforce cease-fire agreements and help restore social order in war-torn lands. By the 1990s the UN was even more willing than in the past to take decisive steps during an international crisis, and its blue-helmeted peacekeepers were common sights around the world.

In February 1993, when Ambassador Albright took her seat in the UN's New York headquarters, the UN had 13 peacekeeping missions underway, with a total of 53,000 troops. Eight of the missions had started after 1989. The UN was in the African nation of Somalia, trying to control private armies that were looting and killing throughout the country. Thousands of miles away in Southeast Asia, UN troops were trying to end a civil war and guarantee peaceful elections in Cambodia. The UN was also in the former republics of Yugoslavia, working to end the conflict that Albright had called the most important to U.S. interests.

When Albright's family lived in Belgrade, Yugoslavia, in 1948, the country was ruled by Communists, but unlike the rest of Eastern Europe, Yugoslavia was independent from the Soviet Union. Under Marshal Tito, the president after World War II, Yugoslavia had some contact with democratic, Western nations, and the Yugoslavs had a slightly better standard of living than most Eastern Europeans. But Yugoslavia had a unique problem: diverse ethnic and religious groups and their historical hatred for one another. Those ethnic tensions fueled the region's problems in the 1990s.

Until 1991, Yugoslavia was one country split into a number of republics, each with some local control. The arrangement was similar to the system of state and federal governments in the United States. In 1990, Communist rule ended in Yugoslavia, and the various republics began to proclaim their independence. In 1991, Croatia and Slovenia were the first to assert their independence, and the others quickly followed suit. Serbia, the most populous republic, and

Montenegro, remained united as Yugoslavia. The former Yugoslav republics created a headache for the world's mapmakers, but the real problems began as ethnic fighting erupted in these newly independent states.

Soon after Croatia became a separate nation, its Serbian minority began to rebel. Yugoslavia supported the Croatian Serbs in their battle to control large segments of Croatia. Fighting continued until 1992, when a United Nations force arrived in Croatia to police a cease-fire agreement. The UN troops set up their command post in Sarajevo, capital of neighboring Bosnia-Herzegovina. Soon after, ethnic fighting broke out in that former Yugoslav republic as well. Three-way battles raged, between Bosnia's Serbs, its Muslims, and its ethnic Croats. Eventually, the Muslims and Croats joined forces against the Serbs.

Under President George Bush, the United States had opposed the Bosnian Serbs, who received military and financial support from the new Serbian-dominated Yugoslav government. America and its European allies relied on diplomacy to try to end the war. The United Nations imposed economic sanctions on Yugoslavia, but the fighting continued. By the end of 1992 the opposing Bosnian forces had destroyed Sarajevo, and the Serbs had massacred many Bosnian Muslims.

The ethnic clash between the Bosnian Muslims and the Serbs, who were Orthodox Christians, was the most appalling aspect of the war. The Serbs practiced what they called "ethnic cleansing"—forcing the Muslims out of Serbian areas and into detention camps, killing and torturing thousands in the process.

This Bosnian Muslim woman balances on the wreckage of her home after it was destroyed by Serbian bombs.

One Serb leader defended the practice by saying "We Serbs need space."[5] To Albright and many other observers, this sentiment and the Serbs' actions were somewhat similar to what the Nazi Germans said and did to Europe's Jews during the Holocaust of World War II.

Albright was also frustrated by the lack of military action by the United States and its European allies to end the slaughter and restore stability to the region. Again, there was an obvious historical parallel, with the way Britain and France let Nazi Germany take over Central Europe—especially Czechoslovakia—in the 1930s.

In April 1993, barely two months on the job as UN ambassador, Albright wrote President Clinton a memo outlining her concerns for Bosnia. By this time, UN troops and humanitarian relief workers were often caught in the fighting between Serbian and Muslim forces. The predominantly Muslim city of Srebrencia had just fallen to Serbian troops and surrendered as the UN watched helplessly on the side.

Albright asked the president to consider air strikes against the Bosnian Serb forces to defend Bosnia's Muslims. If European countries would not join the mission, then the United States should act alone. The UN had already authorized "all measures necessary" to ensure that relief aid reached the beleaguered Muslims. "We should not turn our backs on our international responsibility."[6]

Albright's letter confirmed her reputation as one of the Clinton administration's strongest advocates for military intervention in Bosnia. Secretary of State Warren Christopher and Clinton himself took a more cautious approach. At the time, the United States did not act against the Serbs.

In one strategy meeting on Bosnia, Albright's frustration again boiled over. General Colin Powell, chairman of the Joint Chiefs of Staff, was Clinton's top-ranking military adviser. He had cautioned against U.S. military intervention in Bosnia, under both Presidents Bush and Clinton. Albright demanded of Powell, "What's the point of having this superb military that you're always talking about if we can't use it?"[7]

The problem was not with the capabilities of the U.S. military; what prevented U.S. action were the larger political issues. Did Clinton want to enter what could become a large-scale war in Yugoslavia? Would the American public support intervention in a part of the world that many did not consider absolutely essential to the country's national security? The painful lessons of the Vietnam War colored all future American deliberations about putting U.S. troops into battle.

But as Albright had often said, her thinking was influenced by World War II, not Vietnam. To her, the issue was more clear-cut: The Serbs were committing genocide, and America had a duty to stop it. Publicly, President Clinton also deplored the ethnic cleansing, but the administration was slow to adopt a specific policy in Bosnia.

Finally, in early May, President Clinton supported a two-prong approach called "lift and strike." The United States would agree to lift an arms embargo on Bosnia. The UN had imposed the embargo on all the former Yugoslav republics in 1991. Ending the embargo meant the Bosnian Muslims could arm themselves against the Serbs. "Strike" referred to limited U.S. air strikes if the Bosnian Serbs didn't back down. But even that policy was short-lived. The European allies were cool to the plan, and Clinton lost enthusiasm for "lift and strike."

In New York, the United Nations on May 6 passed a resolution calling for an immediate end to the fighting in Bosnia. Albright denounced the Serbian leaders for refusing to accept a peace plan drafted by former Secretary of State Cyrus Vance and Britain's

Lord David Owen. "Once again, the Bosnian leadership has thumbed its nose at the values that every one in this room holds dear."[8] But with the failure of "lift and strike" to become reality, the Serbs were again free to commit atrocities against the Muslims of Bosnia—at least for the time being.

While Albright was pushing for intervention in Bosnia, she and the rest of the Clinton foreign-policy team were also busy defining the administration's general philosophy for foreign policy. On May 3, Albright appeared before various subcommittees of the House of Representatives and outlined a new approach. The ambassador talked at length about "collective security": America had to work with other countries, often through the United Nations, to ensure security around the world and protect America's vital interests.

Albright realized that some members of Congress might resist expanding America's global military role in a series of small, multinational police actions. But she was convinced that America had a major responsibility as the world's only superpower in an often-chaotic era. "Anyone in this room," she said, "or elsewhere in this country who thinks that what occurs in Bosnia or Somalia or Cambodia is too distant to concern Americans—or has nothing to do with U.S. security—has a very narrow view of economics, politics, and morality and has not learned the lessons of history."[9]

Collective security, Albright continued, does not only require military solutions to conflict, but should also include humanitarian aid and the imposition of economic sanctions on an aggressor nation. Whatever actions were needed, America had to act on its traditional sense of morality, as the country's values "... simply will not permit us to stand aloof from massive human suffering, whether caused by natural or man-made sources."[10]

The policy that Albright articulated that day, and expanded on in the weeks to come, was dubbed "assertive multilateralism." The United States, acting multilaterally with other nations, would respond quickly to confrontation. The country would try to use preventive diplomacy whenever possible, Albright said in another session with congressional committees. But when diplomacy could not prevent or end a conflict, the cost of stability "... will include U.S. forces with attendant potential loss of life."[11]

That potential loss of American lives bothered some members of Congress, especially if the deaths resulted from the incompetence of another country's forces on an international peacekeeping mission. In general, Congress thought Clinton's assertive multilateralism was too ambitious.

Just a few months into Clinton's presidency, Albright seemed to be part of a team with few foreign-policy successes. Finally, in late June, she and the president won bipartisan support on a military action. The foreign leader who defined "evil" for many Americans, Iraq's Saddam Hussein, had once again lashed out at the United States, and Clinton was determined to respond forcefully.

CHAPTER 8

"We also bear special responsibility for international peace and security"

STATE DEPARTMENT DISPATCH, 4/12/93

The 1991 Persian Gulf War introduced most Americans to Saddam Hussein, the dictatorial leader of Iraq. In the complex world of Middle Eastern politics, the United States had supported Saddam in his eight-year war with Iran, in a real-life example of an old saying: "The enemy of my enemy is my friend." Iran had earned America's wrath with the 1980 hostage crisis and its ongoing support of international terrorism.

By 1990, however, Saddam had evolved into the bully of the Middle East—with a million-man army at his disposal. He sent his troops into neighboring Kuwait and was menacingly close to Saudi Arabia, America's strongest Arab ally and the world's leading producer of oil. President George Bush, building a multinational military coalition, led the challenge to Saddam's aggression. The Persian Gulf War was the result.

After the U.S.-led forces drove Iraq from Kuwait, a debate continued on a political level. Why not advance all the way to Baghdad, Iraq's capital, and drive Saddam from power? But General Colin Powell and other advisers told President Bush the goal of eliminating Saddam was not worth a prolonged war and the possible loss of many American lives. The war ended with Saddam defeated in battle but still in power.

After the war, Saddam continued to cause trouble in the Middle East, defying UN personnel who came to inspect the country's arsenal, killing ethnic minorities in the country's border regions, and constantly antagonizing the United States. In the last days of the Bush administration, Iraqi radar sites targeted U.S. jets patrolling the skies over Iraq, and President Bush responded with attacks on antimissile sites and a plant suspected of making nuclear weapons. When he took office, President Clinton said he planned to continue America's tough stance against Saddam.

Clinton had the chance to show his resolve in June 1993. Two months earlier, former president Bush had visited Kuwait, and Kuwaiti officials had uncovered a terrorist attempt to assassinate him. When Clinton had evidence that Iraq sponsored the planned assassination, he moved quickly. On June 26, U.S. ships in the Persian Gulf launched twenty-three missiles at the Iraqi intelligence headquarters in Baghdad in retaliation for the attempt on Bush's life.

The next day, Madeleine Albright asked for a rare Sunday session of the United Nations Security Council. She wanted to explain to the council, and the world, why the United States had attacked Iraq. She described how U.S. intelligence sources had found evidence linking Iraq to the plot. "Even by the standards of an Iraqi regime known for its brutality against its neighbors and its own people, this is an outrage."[1]

Albright cited the UN Charter, which gives every member nation the right of self-defense. In this case, even though the assassination failed, America was justified in taking military action. "In our judgment," she said, "every member here today would regard an assassination attempt against its former head of state as an attack against itself and would react. . . . Our response has been proportional and aimed at a target directly linked to the operation against President Bush. It was designed to damage the infrastructure of the Iraqi regime, reduce its ability to promote terrorism, and deter further acts of aggression against the United States."[2]

Separately, Albright met with an Iraqi representative, Nizar Hamdoon, and warned him that if Iraq retaliated for the U.S. missile attack, President Clinton would launch another attack. Hamdoon accused America of blackmail and of acting on false evidence, but Iraq did not escalate the situation with a military response.

The untested Clinton foreign-policy team looked stronger, more decisive, after the swift response to the Iraqi plot. But other international problems the team had inherited from the Bush administration were less clear-cut than the situation with Iraq. Attacking the dreaded Saddam was bound to score points with the American public, especially if no American lives were at stake. Finding an effective policy for one of the world's most troubled countries, Somalia, would not be as easy.

America's involvement in Somalia started in December 1992, when U.S. forces took the lead in a humanitarian mission to the East African nation. The Somali government collapsed in 1991, and chaos quickly swept the country. Small private armies with ties to leaders called warlords rampaged throughout Somalia, fighting each other and destroying the countryside. The civil war, along with a severe drought, led to mass starvation.

Across America, television news reports showed the devastating effect of the famine. As many as 3,000 people died every day. The United Nations drafted plans for a massive airlift of food. President Bush launched Operation Restore Hope, the American effort to help the UN distribute the food in and around Mogadishu, the capital of Somalia.

In May 1993 most of the U.S. troops pulled out, but the situation in Somalia was far from calm. The next month, Somali militia ambushed UN peacekeepers, killing twenty-three soldiers. The Somalis were loyal to a leading warlord, Mohammed Aidid. In retaliation, the remaining U.S. troops in Somalia attacked Aidid's forces. To justify the attack, President Clinton said, "Aidid's forces were responsible for the worst attack on UN peacekeepers in three decades."[3]

Not all Americans, however, welcomed the increasing U.S. military role in Somalia. Congressional leaders spoke out against the American presence and wondered what would happen once UN and U.S. forces left. Albright, on a trip to Somalia in July, said the UN was working to rebuild the country's political system and its infrastructure of roads and public buildings, but that the media paid more attention to the ongoing violence.

The ambassador also had little use for the warlords. "The warlords had better get their act together," she said. "They are doing nothing to help their country."[4]

Albright's words, however, carried little weight, as Aidid and the other warlords continued to clash. The UN forces could not prevent their destruction, and many Americans were reluctant for the United States to become more involved. In August, four U.S. soldiers died driving over a remote-controlled mine, further adding to the tension.

Once again Albright asserted that the United States had a crucial role to play in Somalia. In an editorial for *The New York Times,* she called Aidid a "renegade" engaging in piracy, and put the blame for the famine on him and his fellow warlords. Despite the dangers of the UN mission in Somalia, America had to remain committed. "The decision we must make is whether to pull up stakes and allow Somalia to fall back into the abyss or to stay the course and help lift the country and its people from the category of a failed state into that of an emerging democracy. For Somalia's sake, and ours, we must persevere."[5]

The military situation in Somalia grew worse, though some humanitarian aid did reach the famished people. Behind the scenes, Albright was one Clinton adviser who recommended sending in special U.S. troops to hunt for Aidid. Clinton finally agreed, but the Army Rangers failed in their mission. An October clash between Aidid's forces and U.S. troops left eighteen Americans dead. President Clinton sent in more troops, but he also promised Congress that all American military forces would leave Somalia by March 1, 1994. Albright and Clinton's policy of "assertive multilateralism" failed to restore order in Somalia.

Albright acknowledged there were problems with the Somali mission, including poorly trained peacekeepers and a lack of coordination between the UN civilian staff and the troops. Also, it was hard to keep the humanitarian part of the mission separate from the fighting, especially when the warlords committed atrocious acts, such as "denying medical aid so that children lie screaming as legs are amputated without anesthesia. . . . "[6]

But such brutality was one reason the United States had to play a role in situations such as Somalia. Once again drawing on her family's experiences in Communist Czechoslovakia, Albright recounted in a speech what her father once said, that too many Czechs had been "willing to let go of core principles and substitute the principles of convenience."[7] America, Albright believed, had to keep its values intact as it pursued its foreign policy.

Another hot spot left by the previous administration was Haiti. Sharing the Caribbean island of Hispaniola with the Dominican Republic, Haiti is one of the world's poorest countries. It was the first Caribbean colony to rebel from its European masters; in 1804 a revolt led by former slaves brought independence. The country, however, always struggled with poverty and political unrest, and starting in 1915, U.S. Marines ran the island for almost twenty years.

After the Americans left, Haiti's politics were controlled by the country's wealthy elite. From 1957 to 1986, the Duvalier family ruled as dictators, using a secret police force to ruthlessly preserve its power. Finally, in 1990, Haiti had its first truly democratic election and voted into office a Roman Catholic priest, Jean-Bertrand Aristide.

Aristide opposed the military, the ruling elite, and even the Catholic Church—any institution that oppressed the majority of Haitians. His philosophy was considered radical, even Communist, and he was unpopular with Haiti's powerful people.

In 1991 a military coup forced Aristide from power, and he fled the country. Haiti became a battleground, as the military and pro-Aristide forces fought. Thousands of Haitians became "boat people," sailing on rickety craft for America, for safety and freedom. Many Americans, however, were not receptive to these refugees, and the Bush administration sent most of them back to Haiti. Some were allowed to stay at Guantanamo, a U.S. naval base in Cuba.

In 1992 an estimated 3,000 Haitians were killed in acts of political violence. When President Clinton took office, he wanted to end Haiti's military dictatorship and restore Aristide to power. But, in the meantime, he retained President Bush's policy on refugees.

At the United Nations, Albright led the fight for sanctions against Haiti's military government. If the country's economy suffered, the generals would be more likely to give in and allow Aristide to return. In

June, UN Security Council Resolution 841 went into effect, banning the shipment of oil to Haiti. Without imported oil, the country could not survive. On July 3, 1993, the military government agreed to let Aristide rule Haiti.

As the date of Aristide's return approached, the United States sent 600 troops to Haiti. Their mission was to help rebuild the country's roads and buildings. But as the ship carrying the troops approached the Haitian shore, supporters of the military government blocked the harbor with boats. Others, carrying weapons, chanted anti-American slogans. The U.S. troops never left their ship.

Tension grew as it became clear that Raoul Cedras, the leader of the military government, was not going to leave office, as he had promised. Ambassador Albright, appearing on television, voiced the Clinton administration's concerns over the events in Haiti. "We have not ruled out anything," she said, implying military force might be necessary. "We are very concerned about the Americans in Haiti and we are concerned about restoring democracy to Haiti."[8]

President Clinton ordered a naval blockade of Haiti, to further tighten the screws on the country's military leaders. The situation deadlocked: Cedras and his cohorts refused to let Aristide take power again, and the United States was hesitant to take military action. Some journalists and Republican leaders saw Haiti as a foreign-policy failure for the Clinton team. The lingering problems in Somalia and Bosnia added to Clinton's image as a weak handler of foreign policy.

But there was one consistency in the Clinton administration: Madeleine Albright's willingness to take a tough stance against the foreign leaders who undermined U.S. interests. To her admirers, Albright was simply practicing hard-nosed diplomacy. Others, including some of her UN colleagues, thought she was abrasive. Still, as she began her second year at the UN, Albright remained highly visible in the Clinton cabinet.

CHAPTER 9

"The road ahead remains steep"

STATE DEPARTMENT DISPATCH, 4/18/94

As the U.S. representative to the United Nations, Madeleine Albright had the duties of attending staff meetings, visiting with foreign leaders, and conferring with other UN ambassadors. She also had the extra responsibilities of a member of the president's cabinet and the National Security Council.

Albright was one of the "Principals," the chief architects of the Clinton administration's foreign policy. Other members included Secretary of State Warren Christopher, Secretary of Defense Les Aspin, and the chairman of the Joint Chiefs of Staff (first General Colin Powell, and then his replacement, General John Shalikashvili). President Clinton and Vice President Al Gore usually participated as well.

At least twice a week, Albright flew back to Washington to attend these meetings. She and the other Principals met in a three-room suite in the basement of the White House called the Situation Room. They discussed Bosnia, or Haiti, or potential international conflicts, then offered suggestions to President Clinton. The Principals did not always agree on what action he should take, and the conversations often dragged on, as the members interrupted each other, arguing among themselves. In these meetings, Albright often played her familiar role of the administration's hawk, advocating strong responses, even military action, to achieve U.S. goals.

Albright's frequent trips to Washington weren't popular with some UN representatives, since they kept her away from meetings and social events in New York. But Albright believed her dual role was good for the UN and for the Clinton administration. "Today I'm in Washington," she told one interviewer, "and when I get back to New York I'll be able to tell them a little more about what our thinking is on a particular issue. And the other way around, I give D.C. real-time knowledge of what's happening at the UN. I see more foreigners per day than anyone else in the administration. I'm on the front line of foreign policy every day, interpreting how people are relating to our foreign policy."[1]

Albright's busy schedule also included trips around the world, such as her visit to Somalia in July 1993. In January 1994 she became the first member of the Clinton administration to visit the former Yugoslav republics. The violence in Bosnia was still intense, and Albright began a swing through Eastern European cities with a stop in Zagreb, capital of Croatia.

Relations between Croatia and the United States had been improving, but Albright was concerned about Croatia's continued military support of Bosnian

Croats. Although the Bosnian Croats and Bosnian Muslims had once fought together against the Serbs, the two groups were now at war. They had negotiated cease-fires, but inevitably the fighting began again. And the Croats, like the Serbs, had conducted ethnic cleansing against the Muslims.

As soon as she arrived in Zagreb, Albright warned the Croats that the United States was considering imposing economic sanctions if Croatia did not stop arming the Croat forces in Bosnia. Albright also discussed the War Crimes Tribunal, which the United Nations had set up in 1993. Albright was one of the major supporters of the tribunal, which would identify and prosecute war criminals who deliberately killed civilians in the various Yugoslav wars. But the UN had to rely on the cooperation of the former Yugoslav republics to make the tribunal work.

The ethnic cleansing carried out against the Bosnian Muslims was the prime example of the war crimes the United Nations wanted to punish. But not all the victims were Bosnian.

In Ovcara, Croatia, Albright visited a mass grave. In a corner of an isolated farm, Albright saw where 200 Croats, patients at a nearby hospital, had been dumped. The bodies were buried beneath worn-out farm equipment and rusted refrigerators. The Croats had been executed by Serb soldiers in 1991; the grave was discovered a year later. Now, UN soldiers guarded the site, to prevent anyone from tampering with evidence before the tribunal heard the case. The UN believed that almost 100 mass graves like this one were scattered across Croatia and Bosnia, holding as many as 4,000 innocent victims of the war.

"This mass grave," Albright said in Ovcara, "is the symbol of the inhumanity that took place. . . . It is a great tragedy that human beings would end their lives in what is ultimately a garbage dump."[2] Albright again held out the threat of economic sanctions if the former Yugoslav republics failed to cooperate with the tribunal.

Not all of the Eastern European trip was as somber as the visit to Ovcara. A few days later, Albright went to Prague and met President Clinton, who was in the middle of his own swing through Europe. Albright's old friend Czech president Vaclav Havel joined her and Clinton for a night on the town, with reporters and video cameras in tow. Clinton entertained the crowd by borrowing a saxophone and playing two songs. But the high-spirited evening was just a short break from Clinton's and Albright's busy schedule.

In the months to come, Albright would continue to throw America's full weight behind the tribunal. She made one of her most passionate arguments for the tribunal in a fitting setting: the U.S. Holocaust Memorial Museum in Washington, D.C.

Albright acknowledged that the Holocaust, the systematic killing of six million Jews during World War II, was much worse than the ethnic cleansing in Bosnia. But both situations raised a similar question: How can humans, who so often can be so compassionate, also sink to the level of beasts? The United States, she argued, as a civilized country, had a duty to do something in Bosnia to try to punish the guilty, just as the Nuremberg trials punished some of the German architects of the Holocaust.

President Bill Clinton, Ambassador Albright, and President Vaclav Havel of the Czech Republic at the start of Clinton and Albright's two-day visit. By all accounts it was a wonderful, relaxing break from the grueling schedules and problems confronting all three of them.

"Most of the victims of the war in Bosnia," Albright said, "like the victims memorialized in this building, [were] not soldiers. . . . They were men and women like you and me—boys and girls like those we know—intentionally targeted not because of what they had done but for who they were."[3]

With her Central European heritage, her father's ties to Yugoslavia, and her academic background,

Albright was always keenly interested in the events in Bosnia. But once again, America's vast foreign-policy interests pulled her attention toward other parts of the world, this time back to Haiti.

President Clinton's critics increasingly spoke out against his policy on Haiti. Refugees were still heading for America, President Jean-Bertrand Aristide was still out of power, and the Haitian military leaders were defiant of the United States and the United Nations. Clinton decided to support even tighter economic sanctions against Haiti, and Albright championed that position at the UN. Haiti's military rulers, she said, "are devoid of honor or patriotism and driven only by greed and mistaken self-interest. . . . We demand an end to the assault on democracy in Haiti."[4]

On May 6, 1994, the UN Security Council voted to impose the stricter economic sanctions that Clinton wanted, and reasserted its desire to see Aristide resume power in Haiti. The UN action had little immediate effect, and the debate over using force to reinstate Aristide grew. But President Clinton had to move slowly; he had just issued a presidential order that steered American policy away from supporting UN peacekeeping missions. American voters were questioning the wisdom of involving U.S. troops in every international conflict.

Jim Ross Lightfoot, a Republican representative from Iowa, expressed to Albright some of the misgivings that he and many Americans had about peacekeeping. "You know, mothers and fathers are not anxious to have their sons and daughters go to war in some foreign country and die for something that they perceive we have no national interest in."[5]

Albright, however, did see a U.S. interest in Haiti. America had to stand up for democratic rule, especially in its own hemisphere. By July 1994, President Clinton was ready to take military action, and Albright persuaded her colleagues at the UN to support his decision, which she endorsed.

On July 31 the Security Council approved Resolution 940, calling for a multinational force, led by the United States, to invade Haiti. In one of her strongest speeches at the UN, Albright blasted Haiti's military leaders and issued them a blunt warning: "You can depart voluntarily and soon, or you can depart involuntarily and soon. The sun is setting on your ruthless ambition."[6]

Raoul Cedras and the other Haitian leaders held power as long as they could. But in September, as U.S. planes carried paratroopers to Haiti, the military leaders agreed to leave. The real threat of American force was enough to finally resolve the crisis.

Albright was still hoping to use American force in Bosnia. The fighting there continued to drag on. A peace plan drafted in June had been approved by everyone but the Bosnian Serbs. In the meantime, the Bosnian Muslims and Croats had launched effective counterattacks against the Serbs. In November the UN approved air strikes against any force that threatened the security of UN peacekeepers or the "safe havens" in Bosnia. The strikes would be carried out by North Atlantic Treaty Organization (NATO) planes. NATO, a military alliance created after World War II, was led by the United States and its European allies. The organization was originally designed to prevent any Soviet attack on Western Europe. Now, NATO was functioning as a police force wherever needed on the continent.

NATO forces did launch an air strike, at an airport used by the Bosnian Serbs. The raid did little damage. Not until August 1995 did NATO launch massive raids against the Serbs, finally convincing the Serbs to discuss peace. Some people wondered why America and its allies had waited so long to take decisive action. Peter Maas, a journalist who covered the war in Bosnia for two years, wrote: "[Clinton and the European leaders] did nothing for more than three years and watched as more than 200,000 people were killed.... Our leaders could have demanded far more in the name of justice, could have done far more in the name of justice, but chose not to."[7]

Albright was one of the few members of the Clinton administration who wanted to do more in the name of justice. Almost two years after the NATO raid on Bosnia, Albright offered her general philosophy on the use of military force: "Rather than feeling it is wrong to interfere, I always believed that if you can stop something early . . . then it's worth doing."[8]

In relations with Iraq, however, there was usually little disagreement among Clinton's advisers or the American public. In October 1994, Saddam Hussein once again stirred trouble, sending an army near the Kuwaiti border. At the UN, Albright advocated a resolution demanding that Saddam withdraw his troops and preparing a military response if he did not. As the Security Council moved slowly on the proposal, the United States acted on its own, sending about 8,000 troops to Kuwait. Finally, the UN backed the American-sponsored resolution. "Let Iraq be warned," Albright said, "and let it fully understand that it should not miscalculate the firmness, unity, and resolve of the Council."[9]

Saddam apparently did understand. He pulled his troops back from the border. America showed its commitment to preserving peace in the Middle East, and the UN was responsive to the country's leadership in international affairs.

CHAPTER 10

"Madeleine is a person of passionate temperament"

NEW YORK TIMES, 11/29/94

With her frequent shuttling between New York and Washington, her trips abroad, and her work on a seemingly never-ending stream of world conflicts, Madeleine Albright's life was increasingly hectic. She perfected the art of taking catnaps wherever she could, learning how to "fall asleep on anything that moves."[1] But despite the long hours and constant traveling, Albright believed she had the best job in the world.

The role of UN ambassador tested her desire to push herself to excel. It drew on the love of international affairs that she cultivated as a child. It let her reach out to others and make a difference in their lives. Albright also received growing attention for her work as Clinton's most outspoken foreign-policy expert— though not all of it was favorable.

Albright's popularity with Bill Clinton was never in doubt. His press secretary, Dee Dee Myers, said

Albright was "a straight talker. She has a way of cutting right to the heart of the matter."[2] And when Albright delivered her most cutting remarks, she did it with White House approval.

Albright made strong statements throughout 1994. When a French official questioned America's stance on the Iraqi military buildup near Kuwait, Albright fired back her own criticism. She said the French official was "ill-informed," and she blasted France for "giving comfort to a brutal dictator who is a repeat offender."[3] At the UN, Albright called remarks by the Iraqi ambassador "the most ridiculous speech ever given by Iraq at the United Nations."[4]

This kind of tough talk drew criticism. Albright, however, took the complaints in stride. When Iraqi officials called her a snake, she appeared at the UN wearing a snake pin on her dress. Another critic called her a witch for supporting continued economic sanctions against Iraq, then underscored the point by sending her a broom. Albright proudly displayed the broom in her office. Though some people at the UN called her "the queen of mean," Albright never backed down. If anything, she seemed to relish the attention she captured.

With President Clinton's approval, Albright was highly visible to the American public. She put on military gear and accompanied Joint Chiefs chairman General John Shalikashvili at peacekeeping training exercises. She spent Thanksgiving with American troops stationed in Haiti. Always relaxed in front of the TV cameras, she made the rounds of the Sunday morning network news shows.

Albright explained her role: "We are in a period of foreign policy when all the rules are different. It's not easy to explain, because the media often do not allow you to have long conversations. But it's important to use whatever time one has to talk to the public, because in a democracy, you have to have public support for policy."[5]

As 1995 began, some journalists were already raising the possibility that Albright could be elevated to secretary of state, if Warren Christopher stepped down. Albright dismissed the suggestion, but she was glad that "people no longer think it is preposterous for there to be a woman secretary of state."[6] Albright, though, had more pressing concerns on her mind. The political climate in Washington had undergone a dramatic change, one bound to affect President Clinton's foreign policy.

In the November 1994 congressional elections, the Republican party took control of both the House of Representatives and the Senate. A conservative senator, Jesse Helms, became chairman of the Senate Foreign Relations Committee. One of the Senate's leading isolationists, Helms declared that much of America's foreign aid was poured down ". . . foreign rat holes to countries that constantly oppose us in the United Nations. . . ."[7] Helms also opposed America's involvement in most UN peacekeeping missions; frequently, he seemed hostile to the whole concept of the organization.

Albright knew that with Helms's increased influence and the Republican majority in Congress, the country would be reexamining its international role and commitments, but she welcomed the upcoming policy debate. The year 1995 was also the 50th anniversary of the United Nations, and Albright began a series of talks addressing the importance of the UN and America's foreign policy.

Appearing before the House International Relations Committee in January, Albright outlined the scope of U.S. involvement in UN peacekeeping missions, calling them just a "tiny fraction" of the country's military activities. In general, she said, "the more able the UN is to contain or end conflict, the less likely it is that we will have to deploy our own armed forces."[8]

In May, Ambassador Albright gave a speech attacking the isolationist impulse of some Americans. Speaking at graduation ceremonies at Barnard College, a women's school affiliated with her alma mater, Columbia, Albright acknowledged that there was increasing turmoil in the world, with civil wars raging and many countries violating their citizens' human rights. Americans, however, could not afford to "pull the covers up over our heads and pretend we do not notice, do not care, and are not affected by events overseas. . . . America is a nation with global interests and responsibilities. Some may find that a burden, but for most Americans, it is a source of great pride."[9]

Albright spoke passionately of America's world responsibilities because she believed in them so deeply. Her words were just as strong when she defended the UN, but even she knew the organization had problems. At 50, the United Nations was dominated by a cumbersome bureaucracy that tolerated wasteful spending and even fraud. The United Nations Children's Fund—UNICEF—recently had lost $10 million through employee theft and mismanagement. Further restricting the UN's finances were delayed contributions from certain member nations. The United States led the list, owing more than $1 billion.

The American reluctance to make timely payments reflected a growing dissatisfaction with the UN among some members of Congress. In the spring of 1995, Senator Helms called for cutting hundreds of millions of dollars in U.S. payments for various ongoing UN programs. In the end, Congress did not cut as much as Helms wanted, but it still budgeted less money than what President Clinton had sought.

American public opinion was also souring on the United Nations. In public-opinion polls, the number of Americans who thought highly of the organization peaked right after the 1991 Persian Gulf War. At that time, 67 percent said the UN was doing a good job. In June 1995 only 42 percent held that positive opinion, while 46 percent said the UN was doing a bad job.

Albright tried to defend and promote the UN in the midst of this hostile public mood. In San Francisco, at ceremonies honoring the 50th anniversary of the United Nations charter, Albright reviewed the historical mission of the UN. ". . . the United Nations Charter was authored by a world emerging from a nightmare, but it was also a world determined . . . to ensure that the horrors just past would not be relived."[10] The world owed it to its children, she said, to nourish the UN's dream of world peace.

As 1995 wore on, Albright had her own problems at the UN. As members of Congress showed less support for the UN, the Clinton administration began to show less support for the UN's secretary-general, Boutros Boutros-Ghali of Egypt. He had held the top position at the UN since 1992. The Clinton administration put much of the blame for the UN's problems on Boutros-Ghali.

When Albright first came to the UN, the secretary-general seemed a little surprised by her blunt style. But by 1994, Albright insisted that she and Boutros-Ghali had a good personal relationship, even if they disagreed on some UN matters. "I really admire him," Albright said.[11]

In 1995, however, mutual dissatisfaction between Boutros-Ghali and the United States boiled over. Early in the year, Boutros-Ghali issued a report summarizing the UN's role in various peacekeeping missions during the previous two years. He criticized the Security Council's role in managing these missions. He also said that certain unnamed countries were wrong to demand UN military intervention while refusing to contribute the money they owed the organization. The secretary-general was clearly referring to the United States.

In response, Albright said Boutros-Ghali seemed to want more power for himself as secretary-general and less for the Security Council, which the United States could not accept. She also criticized the report for assessing blame in failed missions. "I think we

United Nations Secretary-General Boutros Boutros-Ghali at the ceremony to celebrate the 50th anniversary of the United Nations.

have to guard against saying that every time there is a success, it is due to the United Nations, and every time there is a failure, it is due to the member states."[12]

By the year's end, the tensions between Boutros-Ghali and Albright worsened. Reporters and UN staff members speculated whether the United States would support Boutros-Ghali if he ran for another five-year term as secretary-general. Because of its position as a permanent member of the Security Council, the United States could single-handedly deny him the second term.

Boutros-Ghali didn't help his cause during a closed session of the Security Council. The council was meeting to discuss a peacekeeping mission in Croatia. Boutros-Ghali told the council members he was upset by a criticism of him that Albright had made earlier, saying he was "shocked by its vulgarity." Albright had called a Boutros-Ghali recommendation "misguided and counterproductive."[13] Those words might not seem harsh, especially since they were spoken by Albright on a subject she felt strongly about. However, in the world of diplomacy, every negative opinion is expressed in the softest terms possible.

Albright then replied to Boutros-Ghali's comment on her "vulgar" speech. She asserted that she and every member of the Security Council had the right to oppose the secretary-general, his response was out of line, and ". . . to use a word like 'vulgar' is unacceptable."[14] The American dissatisfaction with Boutros-Ghali reached its peak the next year, and President Clinton agreed not to support him for a second term.

After a string of controversies, Ambassador Albright was looking forward to getting away from New York and Washington to attend the Fourth World Conference on Women. Sponsored by the UN, the conference examined social and economic issues that affect women. But even the conference became a political topic in Congress.

The conference was being held in Beijing, China. Some senators and representatives disliked China's human-rights policies and wanted America to boycott the conference. President Clinton, however, supported America's attendance, and in September, Albright led the U.S. delegation to Beijing.

The United States had a number of positions to promote at the conference, including the need to end violence against women. The war in Bosnia had highlighted the use of rape as a tool of war, and Albright wanted the world's male leaders to confront this fact, as well as the more typical domestic violence women face every day. She also wanted to explore ways to ensure proper medical care and educational opportunities for women, and to get men more involved in their families.

Among the U.S. delegation were Geraldine Ferraro, Albright's "student" during the 1984 presidential campaign, and First Lady Hillary Rodham Clinton, who gave an address to open the conference. Albright spoke as well, calling on other countries to help the United States in achieving equal rights for the world's women.

> *Let us strive for the day when every young girl, in every village and metropolis, can look ahead with confidence that their lives will be valued, their individuality recognized, their rights protected, and their futures determined by their own abilities and character.*[15]

The Conference on Women was a forum for many issues. These Tibetan women protest their enforced political silence by China as a crowd gathers to lend support.

Before the conference, a reporter asked Albright if she thought most women didn't like foreign policy, even though it obviously impacted their lives. Albright said she didn't think so. "The problem," she said, "is that it's very difficult for women to be respected in foreign affairs. . . . Even at my level—and I feel that I've finally made it—you have to prove every day that you know what you're talking about."[16]

Albright, as a scholar, policy adviser, and UN ambassador, had made it, but she still had one more promotion ahead of her.

CHAPTER 11

"We have no permanent enemies, only permanent principles"

PREPARED STATEMENT TO CONGRESS, 1/8/97

During the election year of 1996, Madeleine Albright continued speaking out about the importance of the United Nations. She also took time to campaign for President Clinton's reelection. In March, she spoke at a campaign rally at Miami's Orange Bowl. The large audience, mostly Cuban-American, cheered Albright as if she were running for office.

Just a few weeks before, Albright had won the gratitude of Florida's Cuban-American community with one of her most stinging public comments. In February, Cuba shot down two civilian planes based in Miami. The planes were owned by Cuban exiles opposed to Cuba's dictatorial leader, Fidel Castro. Cuba is one of the world's few remaining hard-line Communist states, and the shooting was the latest in a long series of conflicts between America and Cuba, dating from 1959, when Castro took power.

At the UN, Albright said, "Frankly, this is not *cojones*, this is cowardice."[1] Her use of a Spanish slang word referring to testicles shocked some diplomats, but the Cubans—and Bill Clinton—appreciated the toughness and humor her words showed. "Probably the most effective one-liner in the whole Administration's foreign policy," the president later said.[2]

At the UN, Albright led the call for economic sanctions against Cuba, but the Security Council was not sympathetic. It merely condemned the attack. Albright's public image, however, soared after the incident.

In some ways, Albright seemed to be preparing the way for a possible change of jobs if Clinton won reelection in 1996. Secretary of State Warren Christopher had already indicated he would probably not stay on for a second term; he had thought about stepping down once before, in 1994. Albright knew she was one of the candidates for the job. For the first time in her public comments, she indicated that she had thought about earning the top spot in America's foreign policy establishment—though she didn't necessarily expect it.

Still, as a self-confessed political animal, Albright knew the importance of winning the support of influential people. Talking tough against Fidel Castro and Cuba was sure to impress Senator Jesse Helms, still a diehard anti-Communist. If she were ever nominated to be secretary of state, Albright could use the backing of the chairman of the Senate Foreign Relations Committee.

In April, going against the wishes of the White House, Albright accepted an invitation from Helms to speak in North Carolina. In her remarks, Albright politely joked with the senator and referred to him as a "true gentleman." She even used one of his favorite expressions to describe their relationship: "one can always disagree without being disagreeable."[3]

As the year went on, Albright won even more respect from Helms for her public battle with Boutros Boutros-Ghali. Unfortunately, the mission to topple the UN secretary-general did not bolster the popularity of Albright or the United States at the UN.

Secretary of State Warren Christopher tried to negotiate a deal with Boutros-Ghali: If the secretary-general did not run for reelection, the United States would support a one-year extension of his term. An angry Boutros-Ghali quickly dismissed the deal. Christopher then publicly announced that the United States would not support Boutros-Ghali for reelection. Christopher made his statement before Albright could discuss the American decision with her associates at the UN.

The whole affair put Albright and America in a bad light. As the year ended, journalists were reporting that the United States was losing influence at the UN. One *Washington Post* reporter observed, "The U.S. opposition to Boutros-Ghali is especially resented at a time when Washington's failure to pay almost $1.5 billion that it owes in back dues is the principal cause of the financial crisis besetting the United Nations." [4]

Despite the resentment, Albright and the United States held firm, and the UN eventually approved Kofi Annan, of Ghana, as the new secretary-general. Some people speculated that the move against Boutros-Ghali was mostly political, designed to win the favor of American voters who opposed the UN. Whatever the motive, not everyone was impressed with the move and Albright's role in it. Lawrence Eagleburger, secretary of state under George Bush, said, "[Albright's] conduct in the Boutros Boutros-Ghali exercise leaves me with serious question about her judgment."[5]

The Boutros-Ghali incident was one of Albright's more controversial actions as UN ambassador. But as President Clinton's first term drew to a close, he, Albright, and the rest of the administration's foreign-policy team had enjoyed their share of diplomatic successes. The United States had restored democracy in Haiti, and the last U.S. troops had left earlier that year. In the former Yugoslav republics, the warring sides had agreed to a cease-fire that was finally holding. American troops, part of a UN peacekeeping mission, were stationed in Bosnia, and the War Crimes Tribunal was in place.

As the November election drew near, the press began speculating even more about Albright's possible promotion to secretary of state. *The New York Times* profiled her in its Sunday magazine, calling her recent activities her "audition" for the new job.

In the article, Albright talked at length about the frustrations of being a woman in the diplomatic world. "There are lots of questions about women that don't come up for men," she said, "like 'How do you stand being alone?' . . . There is this slight sense that women have to be saints or Joan or Arc, and it's not always possible."[6]

Albright had always succeeded in a predominantly man's world, and many American women wanted to see her become the first female secretary of state. Given that, influential women's organizations were understandably angry after Clinton won reelection and an unnamed White House official told the media that Albright was not among Clinton's top choices for the post. The leading candidates were former Democratic senators Sam Nunn and George Mitchell, and Richard Holbrooke, a former assistant secretary of state.

In a meeting with Vice President Al Gore, representatives from the women's groups reacted strongly to the suggestion that Albright was not really in contention for the job. Said one leader at the meeting, "The comments about Madeleine were not at all appropriate, given her expertise."[7]

President Clinton was also displeased with the remarks. After his long relationship with Albright, he knew her abilities. And he also knew the politics of the situation: Women had backed him over the Republican presidential candidate, Bob Dole, by a large percentage. Clinton did not want to alienate such an important group of voters. And one of his most trusted advisers also backed Albright: the First Lady. Hillary Rodham Clinton had traveled with Albright, consulted her on foreign affairs, and thought she was right for the secretary of state.

On December 5 the president announced his historic appointment of Madeleine Albright as the first woman to serve as secretary of state. After assuring the media he chose her for her talents, not merely to make history or to satisfy women's groups, he did add: "Am I proud that I got the chance to appoint the first woman secretary of state? You bet. My momma's smiling down at me now."[8]

During her remarks at the press conference, Albright talked about her well-known family background as a Czech refugee and the duties that lay ahead for her and the rest of the foreign-policy team. She also addressed her daughters, with whom she had studied at the breakfast table so many years before, and whom she had inspired with her years of hard work. "To my daughters, Alice, Kathy, and Anne—who is here—all I can say is that all your lives I've worried where you were and what you were doing. Now, you will have the chance to worry about me."[9]

In the following days, Washington and the world responded to Albright's nomination, generally in a positive way. One columnist said: "She is certain to

Albright with her daughters Alice, Anne, and Kathy

bring an energy and forcefulness to the job that has been lacking for much of Clinton's first term."[10]

In Britain, some press reports compared her to Margaret Thatcher, that country's former prime minister. Thatcher's blunt, hard-nosed approach to politics earned her the nickname "the Iron Lady." A German diplomat said Clinton "could not have made a better choice from a German and European point of view."[11] And Israel welcomed Albright as a friend who often defended its position on events in the Middle East.

Naturally, there was also criticism of Albright and the appointment. As UN ambassador, Albright had clearly marked herself as a supporter of American intervention in world affairs—with military force, if necessary. Not everyone appreciated that stance. Albright's " 'passion' for activism," one newspaper editor wrote, "does not seem to be attached to or controlled by a clear overarching strategy." That lack of strategy was a "recipe for disaster."[12]

The naysayers, however, were barely heard above the increasing support for Albright. Her newfound friendship with Jesse Helms almost guaranteed that her nomination would face no problems in the Senate, and on January 23, 1997, Albright was officially sworn in as the United States secretary of state.

Albright moved into her office at "Foggy Bottom," the nickname for the State Department. (The department's headquarters are located in a part of Washington that was once swampland often covered with fog.) The secretary met with her staff and encouraged them to come to her directly with ideas. "Don't ignore me just because I'm secretary of state," she told them.[13]

But Albright also wanted her assistants to know she had her own way of doing things and was definitely in charge. At a meeting with senior staff, she said: "You might find that it takes a while getting used to me. I have to warn you I have a way of disregarding the bureaucratic structure and going to people directly."[14] Albright had shown that inclination at the UN, where she was known to go over the heads of her associates in the Security Council and talk directly to their leaders at home.

Albright seemed to adjust quickly to her job and, as always, relished talking about the country's foreign-policy goals. But just two weeks into the job, *The Washington Post* released a surprising story about the new secretary. The information became front-page news, drawing attention from Albright's diplomatic post. The story detailed events about her past that even she didn't know.

CHAPTER 12

"My life has been enriched and strengthened by my heritage and my past"

PRESS RELEASE, 7/3/97

Living as a Czech exile in London during World War II, Madeleine Albright knew firsthand the horrors of that long, devastating war. But as terrible as the battles and bombings were, World War II was also the setting for one of the worst crimes against humanity ever committed—the deliberate, detailed destruction of Jewish people.

Nazi leader Adolf Hitler called his plan "the Final Solution." Hitler had an intense, insane hatred of Jewish people, thinking they had caused all of Germany's problems after World War I. This anti-Semitism was a key part of Hitler's political philosophy.

Many Germans—and other Europeans—shared Hitler's passionate animosity. Loyal Nazis unquestioningly carried out Hitler's plan to imprison, torture, and murder Jews, as well as Gypsies, homosexuals, Communists, and other perceived enemies of Germany. The Jews, however, were a primary target of their systematic killing, which became known as the Holocaust.

Hitler's Final Solution was appalling in its rational approach to genocide. It was, historian A.J.P. Taylor wrote, "the application of advanced modern science to evil ends. Antisemitism and all the talk about race was supposed to be scientific. . . . Chemists devised the most scientific forms of extermination. Doctors tortured the Jews for allegedly medical ends and ransacked their bodies. Skilled technicians built the death camps and perfected the incinerators."[1]

For the Jews who survived the Holocaust, the memories were permanent scars, like the numbers tattooed onto their arms when they arrived at death camps. To endure the camps, one survivor wrote, "the soul had to grow calluses. . . . Pain, pity, grief, horror, revulsion, and approval, if admitted in their normal immediacy, would have burst the receptive capacity of the human heart."[2]

As a scholar and a survivor of Hitler's attempt to dominate Europe, Albright understood the depravity of the Holocaust. Her famous "Munich mind-set" guided much of her thinking on foreign policy: Strong countries like America had a responsibility to prevent aggressor nations from bullying other countries. Moral people had the duty to prevent new holocausts, new attempts at genocide.

In 1994, when Albright visited the American Holocaust Museum and talked about the Bosnian War Crimes Tribunal, she didn't realize how deeply her family's background intersected with the grotesque events remembered at the museum. But after February 1997, she knew.

On February 4, *The Washington Post* ran this headline: "Albright's Family Tragedy Comes to Light." Michael Dobbs, a *Post* reporter who covered the State Department, had been researching a story on the secretary's early life. He went to the Czech Republic, pored through historical documents, and talked to people who knew Albright's family. Dobbs uncovered strong evidence that Josef and Mandula Korbel, Albright's parents, were Jews who converted from Judaism to Catholicism when Albright was a child. They never told Albright her true heritage, nor did they tell her that three of her grandparents and other relatives died in the infamous Nazi death camps of World War II.

The news stunned Albright. She had grown up a Catholic, baptized and confirmed in the church (though she later became a Protestant when she married Joe Albright). Her grandparents, she had been told, had died during the war, though her parents never said how. Being so young at the time, Albright never questioned her parents about her grandparents' deaths. "I had a story," she said, "and there were no gaps in the story, and as a child, if there are no gaps, you don't ask questions."[3]

A few days after its initial report, the *Post* published Dobbs's complete account of Albright's family history. Korbel and his wife were never devoutly religious, and at some point before or during the war, they converted to Catholicism.

Less than two years old when she left Czechoslovakia for England, Albright had no memories of her three surviving grandparents (her mother's father had already died of an illness). When Madeleine was older, the Korbels told her about long-ago family Christmases and Easter celebrations—all of which had never happened. But the stories helped convince their daughter she came from a Catholic family.

Josef and Mandula probably did not know exactly what happened to the relatives they left behind in Czechoslovakia, but they knew the fate of Jews and other Nazi "enemies." In 1944, the Czech radio service in London, which Josef Korbel ran, broadcast a report on the slaughter of thousands of Jews at Terezin, a concentration camp in Czechoslovakia. "This new crime of the Nazis is incredible in its inhumane horror," the broadcast said. "Those who took part in carrying out such bestialities will not escape justice."[4]

More than 50 years later, Albright learned that her grandfather, Arnost Korbel, had died at Terezin in 1942. Two years later, his wife, Olga, died at Auschwitz, the most notorious death camp. Albright's maternal grandmother, Anna Spieglova, also died at a camp, though the evidence wasn't clear where.

Albright's new family history quickly became a major news story, receiving more coverage than her diplomatic goals at her new job. Along with the story came questions: How did Albright feel about this revelation? What did she think about her parents keeping this secret from her? Did she have any inkling of her heritage? America's Jewish community was especially interested in the story, as it raised many issues about the choices some Jews had made during and since that troubled period of their history.

Albright's first response was to defend and praise her parents' actions. "I think my father and mother were the bravest people alive," she told *The New York Times*. "They dealt with the most difficult decision anyone could make. I am incredibly grateful to them, and beyond measure."[5]

The revelations of her family history saddened Albright, as she learned how her grandparents had died. But in many ways the news did not change her. "I always thought the Holocaust was one of the most horrifying acts in human history. . . . I have always been opposed to totalitarianism. In terms of my basic beliefs, I haven't had to change anything. I have always been proud of my heritage. I am now even prouder of my heritage. . . . "[6]

The Jewish issue, however, created problems for Albright, as her initial comments about the report were sometimes inconsistent. When Michael Dobbs first asked Albright if she had any idea about her Jewish heritage, she said she had received letters from people saying her family was Jewish, but the letters lacked real proof and often had many facts wrong, so Albright ignored them.

Later, Albright told some reporters that she was totally surprised by the news of her Jewish roots. But then she said what she meant was that she was surprised to learn that her grandparents had died in the death camps, not that she might be Jewish. Some Jewish Americans thought Albright was not telling the truth. Frank Rich, a prominent *New York Times* columnist and a Jew, asked: "What smart, serious, sensitive student of history, let alone a Nazi refugee, makes no effort to find out how her grandparents died?"[7]

The Albright affair also raised a larger issue. After World War II, many Jewish Americans found it helpful to downplay their heritage if they wanted to succeed in a country that had its own degree of anti-Semitism. "Her family's obliteration of its Jewish past . . . wouldn't resonate so loudly if it didn't awaken guilty memories in many other American homes," wrote Rich.[8]

Albright might have learned about her family earlier. On a 1994 trip to Europe, she gave a press conference in Prague. In the audience was Dagmar Simova, the cousin who lived with Albright and her family during and after World War II. Since parting from the Korbels in 1948, Simova had remained in Czechoslovakia, enduring life in a Communist country and raising a family. She wanted to renew contact with her cousin, and she passed a note to one of Albright's bodyguards. Albright never got it.

Unlike her cousin, Simova knew about the family's Jewish roots and how their grandparents had died. Her children also knew, unlike Albright's three daughters. Said Simova, "I never for a moment suspected that she did not know."[9]

Then, in 1995, a Holocaust research center in Prague published a list of the more than 77,000 Jews taken from Czechoslovakia to the death camps. The names of Josef Korbel's parents were on the list. The mayor of Prague sent Albright a letter containing this information, but it never reached her.

Within a few weeks of the initial *Washington Post* story, Albright was upset that people questioned what she had known about her past. She told Frank Rich, "I'm deeply hurt that people think I'm lying."[10] She apologized for not being clear in her first statements, and she admitted she wasn't totally surprised to learn she was Jewish. "I had hints along the way. I feel pretty stupid. It's like seeing a bunch of dots and when a person puts it all together it makes sense. . . . I had not been sensitive enough to signs that my background was different than I thought it was."[11]

Kathy Silva, Albright's sister, and her brother John went to Prague to investigate the story for themselves. They were also unaware of the family's background. Albright's busy schedule prevented her from going there until July, when she made an eight-day swing through Europe. Albright visited her hometown for the first time as secretary of state, and she spent her first hours at the city's Jewish landmarks, including a cemetery and the Pinkas Synagogue.

Inside the synagogue, the names of all the Czech Jews who died in the death camps are carved into the walls. Albright searched the walls until she found the names she was looking for: Arnost and Olga Korbel.

Later, Albright fought back tears as she described her visit to the synagogue, which she had been to the year before with First Lady Hillary Rodham Clinton. "At that time," Albright said:

I was deeply moved by the thousands of names carved on the wall. But because I did not know my own family history then, it didn't occur to me to look for the names of grandparents or other family members. Tonight, I knew to look for those names—and their image will be forever seared into my heart. . . . Now that I am aware of my own Jewish background—and the fact that my grandparents died in concentration camps—the evil of the Holocaust has an even more personal

meaning for me, and I feel an even greater deter-
mination to ensure that it will never be forgot-
ten. . . . I leave here tonight with the certainty
that this new part of my identity adds something
stronger, sadder, and richer to my life.[12]

In September, on a return trip to Prague, Albright visited the site of the Terezin concentration camp, located just north of the Czech capital. About a week later, she was in Jerusalem on her first official visit to the Middle East as secretary of state. Like other secretaries before her, she visited Yad Vashem, a memorial for the victims of the Holocaust. She laid a wreath and relit a memorial flame, but her presence was not just ceremonial; the Holocaust memorial now had personal meaning. She spoke briefly after her visit: "The history remembered here . . . is a history of unbearable sadness, unrelieved suffering and unbelievable cruelty. That is why this memorial and this museum are so troubling, and why it matters so much that they continue to trouble us."[13]

CHAPTER 13

"Adapting to change is never easy"

ADDRESS AND Q&A TO COUNCIL ON FOREIGN RELATIONS, 9/30/97

The reports on her family background gripped Madeleine Albright's attention, but she couldn't let the issue distract her from her job. As secretary of state, Albright was ultimately responsible for 250 overseas diplomatic offices and a budget of more than $19 billion, though the department's budget had shrunk in previous years. Those cutbacks resulted in more than 2,000 layoffs, reductions in foreign assistance, and weakened morale among the staff.

Albright wanted to assure everyone that she understood the problems the department faced, and she was not going to isolate herself. On her first day in office, she ate in the State Department cafeteria, a symbolic gesture of her concern.

In early February, the secretary made her first official trip, but instead of leaving the country, she went to Houston to deliver a speech at Rice University. She was eager to fulfill two of her self-imposed goals: convince Republicans to support her proposals and clearly explain foreign policy to the American people. As she said in her speech, "I will do my best to talk about foreign policy not in abstract terms, but in human terms, and in bipartisan terms; I consider this vital because in our democracy, we cannot pursue policies abroad that are not understood and supported here at home."[1]

To build that bipartisan approach, while in Houston Albright visited former president George Bush and former secretary of state James Baker. Both men were Republicans respected in foreign-policy matters, so gaining their support could help Albright and President Clinton win the backing of Republicans in Congress.

In the next few months, Albright stepped up her public-relations campaign. On February 20, she became the first secretary of state to hold a Web chat on the Internet. Her comments reached students in all fifty states and in schools in forty-seven foreign countries. She also set up her own E-mail address, "secretary@state.gov," and received about 200 messages a week. This electronic correspondence was in addition to the 2,700 letters sent to her every week.

Turning from public relations to politics, Albright continued to improve her relationship with Senator Jesse Helms. In April she went with Helms to Wingate College, the North Carolina school the senator attended as a young man. Once again, as she had done in 1996, Albright used humor to flatter Helms. But she had a larger policy goal as well: She hoped to persuade Helms to support a treaty to end the use of chemical weapons.

The Chemical Weapons Convention was endorsed by most major countries, but Helms had refused to let the treaty leave his Foreign Relations Committee. The treaty needed approval by the full Senate for the United States to be a party to it. After Albright discussed the horror of chemical weapons during her Wingate speech, Helms agreed to let the treaty move to the Senate for debate. A few weeks later, thanks to strong lobbying by Albright and President Clinton, the Senate approved the Chemical Weapons Convention.

Albright sought Helms's support on another issue—the treatment of women. In March, Albright campaigned to win Senate backing for a United Nations treaty ending discrimination against the world's women. Like the Chemical Weapons Convention, this treaty had been stuck in the Foreign Relations Committee, never receiving a hearing in the Senate.

On March 12, International Women's Day, Albright said the United States had a "mission" to improve the treatment of women. "It is the right thing to do," she said, "and frankly it is the smart thing to do. . . . common sense tells us that true democracy is not possible without the full participation of women."[2]

Two weeks later, at the Wingate College appearance with Helms, Albright made a direct appeal for the Senate to ratify the treaty. Unlike the chemical weapons treaty, however, Albright was not able to win an immediate concession from Helms.

Although domestic politics were important, Albright's main responsibilities were abroad, and her first foreign trip as secretary, in mid-February, took her to nine countries in eleven days. The highlight of the trip was a stop in China.

Before Albright took office, some foreign-policy experts questioned her ability to deal effectively with the Chinese, given that she had little background in Asian affairs. China, the experts warned, would present some of America's greatest foreign-policy challenges.

With its huge population of more than 1.2 billion and a rapidly growing economy, China might one day be an important trading partner for America. But China is also the world's major Communist country, with an arsenal of nuclear weapons that make it a potential foe. As China modernized its economy, its politics remained repressive. Political freedom was scarce in China, and the government's authoritarian policies created tension between China and the United States.

During her trip to China's capital, Beijing, Albright acknowledged China's importance to America. "Our relations with China," she said, "are key to our stability and prosperity in the twenty-first century."[3]

The Chinese also realized the need for good relations with America. To meet with the secretary of state, China's leaders interrupted funeral plans for the country's former leader, Deng Xiaoping, who died on February 19. Albright and the Chinese discussed a range of topics: nuclear arms, trade issues, human rights. When she returned to America, the secretary said: "We have some things we disagree about . . . but what I got a sense of is that [the Chinese and the Americans] understand that this is going to be a critical relationship. . . . "[4]

Even more than when she was UN ambassador, Albright had to juggle a huge array of foreign-policy issues. In Asia, she had to deal not only with China but also the lingering hatred between China's ally, North Korea, and the democratic country of South Korea. In Cambodia, the scene of genocide committed by a Communist government against its own people, rival factions were struggling for control of the government. Meanwhile, in Europe, the former Yugoslav republics were at peace, but the region was still not completely stable. And the rest of Central and Eastern Europe was still adjusting, psychologically and economically, to life after communism.

The United States wanted a closer relationship with some of the former Soviet-controlled countries. The Clinton administration wanted three of those nations—Poland, Hungary, and the Czech Republic—to join NATO. Russia, although now more democratic and pursuing a capitalist economy, was still wary of NATO. Some Russians feared that the United States wanted to dominate their country. Albright, who strongly supported the expansion of NATO, worked hard to convince the Russians that America only wanted a secure, free Europe, not domination.

America's goal, Albright said, was "an integrated Europe—one that included, not excluded, Russia."[5] Ensuring stability in Central and Eastern Europe would ultimately help the Russians, too. The Russians reluctantly accepted the NATO expansion once the United States guaranteed them some input in certain future NATO operations.

In July the members of NATO met in Madrid, Spain, to vote on admitting the three new members, as of 1999. Albright was thrilled with the result and went to the Czech Republic to welcome her homeland into the alliance. The day after her emotional trip to Prague's Pinkas Synogogue, Albright addressed the Czechs, including President Vaclav Havel.

Albright recounted her many trips to Prague since the Velvet Revolution of 1989. "But nothing," she said, "compares to the feeling of coming to my original home, Prague, as the secretary of state of the United States, for the purpose of saying to you: Welcome home. For with the news from Madrid this week, you are coming home *in fact* to the community of freedom that you never left *in spirit*."[6]

Throughout the summer, Albright continued to travel around the world, introducing herself to foreign leaders and spelling out President Clinton's policies. One crucial issue was the strained relationship between Israel and the Palestinian Arabs living within its borders. Some observers wondered if her new knowledge about her Jewish roots would affect her objectivity in the region. But Albright had always been a strong defender of Israel, as most American diplomats have been since the country's founding in 1948. Americans played a large role in the creation of Israel, which is a democratic state and a military ally. The Israelis have faced almost constant military threat from its Arab neighbors. But since the Carter administration, U.S. leaders have worked hard to bring peace to the region and try to balance the interests of Palestinians with Israeli security.

The Palestinians claim that they deserve a homeland, too, and they have struggled to gain control of Israeli territory they feel belongs to them. Israel, meanwhile, asserts it has historical rights to all the lands it occupies. The conflict has led to years of violence and terrorism in Israel and neighboring Lebanon. Finally, in 1994 and 1995, Israel granted the Palestinians limited self-rule within Israel's borders. Those agreements had come with American diplomatic help. But the violence continued, as extremists on both sides resented the new Israeli-Palestinian cooperation. When Secretary Albright went to Israel for her first official visit, talks between the Israelis and Palestinians had broken down, and she hoped to jump-start the peace process.

New terrorist violence did not help her cause. Two suicide bombings in Jerusalem over the summer killed fifteen people. Another bombing occurred just before Albright arrived, and she visited some of the victims in the hospital. She saw Jewish and Arab patients being tended by Jewish and Arab nurses, and she thought, "If these two people can hurt and heal together, surely they can also live together."[7] But by the end of her visit, Albright did not see any diplomatic movement that rewarded her faith.

Albright had to walk a fine line: assure Israel of America's continued support, while addressing the rights of the Palestinians. Speaking to an Israeli audience, the secretary said, "America's commitment to Israel's security is and will always be rock solid."[8] Then, during a radio address to the Palestinians, Albright said Israel should end some of its more oppressive policies, such as taking away Palestinian land and expanding Jewish settlements. She met with the two leaders involved, Benjamin Netanyahu of Israel and Yassir Arafat of the Palestinians. The two sides seemed reluctant to hold meaningful discussions. After the trip, a disappointed Albright said, "The crisis of confidence there is worse than I thought—it's fairly tattered."[9] She held further meetings with the two leaders at the end of 1997, once again trying to reopen peace talks. Israel did promise to turn over more of its land to the Palestinians, though it expected Arafat to do more to combat the terrorism directed at Israelis.

Albright, however, could not stay solely focused on this one region of the Middle East. To the north, America's old nemesis, Saddam Hussein, was once again stirring up trouble. On September 30, the secretary had assured one audience that Saddam "remains in a strategic box."[10] But even within that box, he had the ability to thumb his nose at the world community, represented by the United Nations. Just a short while later, Saddam tried to prevent UN weapons inspectors from entering Iraq. President Clinton said Saddam had no right to control where the inspectors went, and in November he began mobilizing forces in the Persian Gulf, threatening to use force to make Saddam cooperate.

Meanwhile, behind the scenes, Albright talked with America's European allies, Russian officials, and Arab leaders to try to end the conflict peacefully. With Russian help, the crisis was prevented—for the moment. By year's end tensions were rising again, as Saddam denied permission to a U.S. member of the UN team to participate in inspections. And certain sites, the Iraqi leader said, were off limits to all UN inspectors. As the conflict carried over into 1998,

Albright once again sought to use diplomacy to settle the issue, while assuring Saddam that the United States was ready to fight if it had to. As always, she projected a tough image while working for peace. Speaking in Jerusalem, the secretary said: "We must stop Saddam from ever again jeopardizing the stability and security of his neighbors with weapons of mass destruction.... if diplomacy runs out we have reserved the right to use force, and if we do so, it will be substantial...."[11]

In the days after that statement, President Clinton sent about 2,000 U.S. Marines into the Persian Gulf, joining warships, personnel, and equipment already in the region. And Albright continued her difficult task of trying to preserve peace while pursuing America's diplomatic objective of keeping Saddam in check. A break in the crisis seemed to come in late February, when UN Secretary-General Kofi Annan traveled to Baghdad. Annan negotiated a deal with Saddam to allow the weapons inspectors back into Iraq.

Reaction in America was mixed. Some Republican senators opposed the deal, while the Clinton administration generally accepted it. But Clinton and Albright did not rule out using the military if Saddam were to change his mind once again. In a television interview, the secretary said: " . . . there have to be clarifications . . . there will be a time of testing as the inspectors go out, verifying that the various aspects of this are in place, and then making sure that Iraq stays in compliance.... we're keeping our forces out there."[12]

CHAPTER 14

"We will not hesitate to lead"

PRESS REMARKS, 1/28/98

The ongoing tension with Iraq marked the anniversary of Madeleine Albright's first year as secretary of state. During that year, she had made history as the first woman to hold that important position; discovered the details of her Jewish roots; and traveled around the globe as America's most visible diplomat. Her popularity soared, both at home and abroad. Albright received hundreds of invitations to address American college students, civic groups, and other organizations. Her busy schedule let her accept only a few. On her missions to countries such as South Africa, she was warmly received by both political leaders and average citizens. During a visit to refugee camps in Uganda and Rwanda, she talked to people in hospitals and schools. Once, she held a young baby in her arms, comforting the child just hours after her mother had been killed. Wherever she went, Albright brought a human touch to American diplomacy.

Most American observers applauded Albright's efforts. Jack Galvin, dean of the Fletcher School of Law and Diplomacy, said, "I think she's had a good first year." But Galvin warned of trouble to come: "There is a lot lying ahead in terms of major issues that are going to dominate the early part of the twenty-first century."[1]

One of those key issues is relations with China. During 1997, Secretary of State Albright and President Clinton had sometimes been criticized for seeming to be too friendly with China, without demanding more reforms within that Communist country. Many Americans were concerned about China's treatment of political prisoners and its continued domination of Tibet. Once an independent nation, this Buddhist homeland of the Dalai Lama has been under Chinese control since 1951. Albright has to somehow balance the concern for human rights with the need for good trade and diplomatic relations with the world's most populous country.

In October, Chinese president Jiang Zemin came to America. It was the first time a Chinese leader had visited America since the Tiananmen Square rebellion of 1989. Hundreds of thousands of Chinese had peacefully protested for democratic reforms. The government responded with a military attack that killed and injured thousands. Before Jiang's trip, Albright outlined the U.S. government's position on China. "Human rights is a major component of our trying to deal with China and having them do it properly," she said. "We will never have a completely normal relationship with them until they have a better human-rights policy."[2]

But Albright sees the other side of the coin as well. "I think it's very important for the American people to understand that it would be at our own loss if we do not engage in a relationship with China—a country that has increasing power and can in fact help us in terms of national security issues. . . ."[3]

Another lingering problem for Albright and the United States is relations between Israel and the Palestinians. She admitted that "1997 was not a good year for the peace process."[4] In February 1998, while in the Middle East to discuss the crisis with Iraq, Albright met once again with Israeli and Palestinian officials, trying to get the peace talks back on track. Before the trip, she said she was not optimistic, because "leaders in the region remain reluctant to make the hard decisions and to offer the flexibility required to reach an agreement." But she was not totally pessimistic, either, since she believed "the majority of all faiths and communities in the region desire peace. . . ."[5]

Albright's background had prepared her for the complexity of issues such as relations with China and the Middle East peace process. Although she could not predict how these matters would be settled, her dedication to learning, democratic values, and human rights, balanced with her tough, direct manner, make her an excellent person to lead American foreign policy into the twenty-first century.

BIBLIOGRAPHY

Books

Albright, Madeleine K. *Poland: The Role of the Press in Political Change.* New York: Praeger, 1983.

——. *The Role of the Press in Political Change: Czechoslovakia 1968.* Ph.D. dissertation, Columbia University, 1976.

Aristide, Jean-Bertrand. *Dignity.* Translated by Carrol F. Coates. Charlottesville, VA: University Press of Virginia, 1996.

Black, Christine, and Oliphant, Thomas. *All by Myself: The Unmaking of a Presidential Campaign.* Chester, CT: Globe Pequot Press, 1989.

Blood, Thomas. *Madam Secretary.* New York: St. Martin's Press, 1997.

Brisch, Hans, and Volgyes, Ivan. *Czechoslovakia: The Heritage of Ages Past. Essays in Memory of Josef Korbel.* Boulder, CO: East Europe Quarterly, 1979.

Brzezinski, Zbigniew. *Power and Principle: Memoirs of the National Security Advisor, 1977-1981.* New York: Farrar, Strauss & Giroux, 1983.

Drew, Elizabeth. *On the Edge: The Clinton Presidency.* New York: Simon & Schuster, 1994.

——. *Washington Journal: The Events of 1973-1974.* New York: Macmillan, 1984.

Ferraro, Geraldine. *My Story*. New York: Bantam Books, 1985.

Goldman, Peter, and Fuller, Tony. *The Quest for the Presidency, 1984*. New York: Bantam Books, 1985.

Kogon, Eugen. *The Theory and Practice of Hell*. Translated by Heinz Norden. New York: Berkley Books, 1958.

Korbel, Joseph. *Twentieth-Century Czechoslovakia: The Meanings of Its History*. New York: Columbia University Press, 1977.

Lyons, Lawrence, and Samatar, Ahmed I. *Somalia: State Collapse, Multilateral Intervention, and Strategies for Political Reconstruction*. Brookings Occasional Papers. Washington, D.C.: The Brookings Institution, 1995.

Maass, Peter. *Love Thy Neighbor*. New York: Alfred A. Knopf, 1996.

Maass, Robert. *UN Ambassador*. New York: Walker and Company, 1995.

Paterson, Thomas G., Clifford, J. Garry, and Hagan, Kenneth J. *American Foreign Policy: A History*. Lexington, MA: D. C. Heath and Company, 1977.

Perusse, Roland I. *Haitian Democracy Restored, 1991-1995*. Lanham, MD: University Press of America, 1995.

Powell, Colin. *My American Journey*. New York: Random House, 1995.

Prados, John. *Keepers of the Keys: A History of the National Security Council From Truman to Bush*. New York: William Morrow & Co., 1991.

Rieff, David. *Slaughterhouse: Bosnia and the Failure of the West*. New York: Simon & Schuster, 1995.

Silber, Laura, and Little, Allan. *Yugoslavia: Death of a Nation*. TV Books, 1996.

Simons, Anna: *Networks of Dissolution: Somalia Undone*. Boulder, CO: Westview Press, 1995.

Taylor, A. J. P. *The Second World War*. New York: Paragon Books, 1975.

Wheal, Elizabeth-Anne, Pope, Stephen, and Taylor, James. *Encyclopedia of the Second World War*. Edison, NJ: Castle Books, 1989.

Wheaton, Bernard, and Kavan, Zdenek. *The Velvet Revolution: Czechoslovakia, 1988–1991*. Boulder, CO: Westview Press, 1992.

Woodward, Susan L. *Balkan Tragedy.* Washington, D.C.: The Brookings Institution, 1995.

Newspapers, Magazines, and Journals
In addition to the specific sources cited in the endnotes, I relied on various issues of *Congressional Quarterly Weekly, Newsweek, The New York Times, Time, U.S. News and World Report, U.S. State Department Dispatch,* and *The Washington Post* for background information, as well as the sources listed below.

Albright, Madeleine K. "The Role of the United States in Central Europe." *Academy of Political Science Proceedings,* Vol. 38, No. 1 (1991), pp. 71–84.

U.S. Congress. House. Subcommittee on Africa of the Committee on Foreign Affairs. *Somalia: Prospects for Peace and Stability.* 103rd Congress, 2nd session, March 16, 1994.

U.S. Congress. Senate. Committee on Armed Services. *Briefing on Bosnia and Other Current Military Operations.* 103rd Congress, 2nd session, February 23, 1994.

NOTES

CHAPTER 1

1. Quoted in Alexander DeConde, *The American Secretary of State* (New York: Frederick A. Praeger, 1962), p.132.
2. Quoted in Thomas G. Paterson, J. Garry Clifford, and Kenneth J. Hagan, *American Foreign Policy* (Lexington, MA: D.C. Heath, 1977), p. 51.
3. Kevin Fedarko, "Clinton's Blunt Instrument," *Time*, October 31, 1994, p. 31.
4. Quoted in ibid.
5. "Shared Resolve in Restoring Democracy in Haiti," *U.S. Department of State Dispatch*, Vol. 5, No. 33 (August 15, 1994), p. 554.
6. Quoted in Matthew Cooper and Melinda Liu, "Bright Light," *Newsweek*, February 10, 1997, p. 23.
7. Ibid.
8. Ibid.
9. Quoted in Barbara Crossette, "A Political Diplomat: Madeleine Korbel Albright," *The New York Times*, December 6, 1996, p. A1.
10. Press Release, Office of the Spokesman, Department of State, January 8, 1997.
11. Press Release, White House Office of the Press Secretary, January 23, 1997.

12. CNN, "Larry King Live," January 24, 1997.
13. Ibid.

CHAPTER 2

1. Michael Dobbs, "Out of the Past," *The Washington Post Magazine*, February 9, 1997, p. 12.
2. Quoted in G.E.R. Gedye, "Czech Rulers Bow But Under Protest," *The New York Times*, October 1, 1938, p. 2.
3. Quoted in Dobbs, p.13.
4. CBS, "60 Minutes," February 9, 1997.
5. Quoted in Nancy Gibbs, "The Many Lives of Madeleine," *Time*, February 17, 1997, p. 58.
6. Quoted in Dobbs, p. 18.
7. Quoted in Steven Erlanger, "Albright Grateful for Her Parents' Painful Choices," *The New York Times*, February 5, 1997, p. A8.
8. Quoted in Elaine Sciolino, "Madeleine Albright's Audition," *The New York Times Magazine*, September 22, 1996, p.67.

CHAPTER 3

1. Quoted in Molly Sinclair, "Woman on Top of the World," *The Washington Post*, January 6, 1991, p. F4.
2. Quoted in Josef Korbel, *Twentieth-Century Czechoslovakia: The Meanings of Its History* (New York: Columbia University Press, 1977), p. 246.
3. Quoted in Dobbs, p. 23.
4. Quoted in Sinclair, p. F4.
5. Quoted in Sciolino, "Madeleine Albright's Audition," p. 104.
6. Quoted in Annie Hill, "Appointee Spent Teen Years in Denver," *The Denver Post*, December 6, 1996, p. A1
7. Quoted in John Brinkley, "Diplomat From Denver," *The Rocky Mountain News*, June 15, 1997, p. 33W.
8. "Kennedy Seeks Campaign Aid in Whistle Stop," *Wellesley College News*, October 16, 1958, p. 5.
9. Quoted in Sinclair, p. F4.

CHAPTER 4
1. Quoted in Sinclair, p. F1.
2. Ibid.
3. Ibid., p. F6.
4. Quoted in Bill Hewitt, "Madam Secretary," *People*, December 23, 1996, p. 47.
5. James B. Bruce, "In Memoriam: Josef Korbel," in *Czechoslovakia: The Heritage of Ages Past, Essays in Memory of Josef Korbel*, Hans Brisch and Ivan Volgyes, eds. (Boulder, CO: East Europe Quarterly, 1979), p. 7.
6. Quoted in Paterson and others, p. 600.
7. Quoted in Cooper and Liu, p. 26.
8. Zbigniew Brzezinski, *Power and Principle: Memoirs of The National Security Advisor, 1977–1981* (New York: Farrar, Strauss & Giroux, 1983), p. 76.
9. CBS, "60 Minutes," February 9, 1997.
10. Zbigniew Brzezinski, *Introduction to Madeleine Albright, Poland: The Role of the Press and Political Change* (New York: Praeger, 1983), p. vi.
11. Quoted in ibid., back cover.

CHAPTER 5
1. As recalled by Madeleine Albright in Sciolino, "Madeleine Albright's Audition," p. 104.
2. Quoted in Sinclair, p. F4.
3. CBS, "60 Minutes," February 9, 1997.
4. Quoted in Sciolino, "Madeleine Albright's Audition," p. 104.
5. Quoted in Sinclair, p. F4.
6. Geraldine Ferraro, *My Story* (New York: Bantam Books, 1985), p. 118.
7. Ibid., p. 255.
8. Quoted in ibid., p. 275.
9. Quoted in Elaine Sciolino, "Dukakis's Foreign Policy Advisor," *The New York Times*, July 26, 1988, p. A16.
10. Quoted in Charlotte Saikowski, "Dukakis's Foreign Policy Outline," *The Christian Science Monitor*, July 27, 1988, p. 3.

11. Ibid.
12. Quoted in Andrew Rosenthal, "Dukakis Questions Bush's Leadership," *The New York Times*, August 6, 1988, p. A7.

CHAPTER 6

1. Vaclav Havel, *Open Letters: Selected Writings, 1965-1990* (New York: Alfred A. Knopf, 1991), p. 395.
2. Ibid., p. 396.
3. Quoted in Sinclair, p. F4.
4. Quoted in Thomas L. Friedman, "Havel's Paradoxical Plea: Help Soviets," *The New York Times*, February 22, 1990, p. A1.
5. Quoted in Sinclair, p. F4.
6. Ibid.
7. Ibid.
8. Quoted in Jacob Heilbrunn, "Albright's Mission," *The New Republic*, August 22–29, 1994, p. 24.

CHAPTER 7

1. Quoted in Dan Balz, "U.N. Post Will Complete Odyssey for Albright," *The Washington Post*, December 23, 1992, p. A10.
2. Quoted in 1992 *CQ Almanac* (Washington, D.C.: Congressional Quarterly Inc., 1993), p. 153A.
3. Mary McGrory, "A Humanist for the Activist," *The Washington Post,* December 29, 1992, p. A2.
4. "Statement at Confirmation Hearings of US Ambassador to the United Nations," *US Department of State Dispatch*, Vol. 4, No. 15 (April 12 1993), p. 231.
5. Quoted in Laura Silber and Allan Little, *Yugoslavia: Death of a Nation* (TV Books, 1996) p. 233.
6. Quoted in Michael R. Gordon, "Twelve in State Department Ask Military Move Against the Serbs," *The New York Times*, April 23, 1993, p. A1.
7. Quoted in Colin Powell, *My American Journey* (New York: Random House, 1995), p. 576.
8. "US Explanation of Vote on UN Resolution 824," *US Department of State Dispatch*, Vol. 4, No. 20 (May 17, 1993), p. 348.

9. "Building a Collective Security System," *US Department of State Dispatch*, Vol. 4, No. 19 (May 10, 1993), p. 332.
10. Ibid., p. 333.
11. "Myths of Peacekeeping," *US Department of State Dispatch*, Vol. 4, No. 26 (June 28, 1993), p. 467.

CHAPTER 8

1. "Excerpts From U.N. Speech: The Case for Clinton's Strike," *The New York Times*, June 28, 1993, p. A13.
2. Ibid.
3. Quoted in Pat Towell, "Risk of Peacekeeping Shown in Battle With Warlord," *Congressional Quarterly Weekly*, June 19, 1993, p. 1590.
4. Quoted in "Somali Leaders Are Accused of Undermining U.N. Efforts," *The New York Times*, July 4, 1993, p. A12.
5. "Yes, There Is a Reason to Be in Somalia," *The New York Times*, August 10, 1993, p. A19.
6. "Agenda for Dignity," *U.S. Department of State Dispatch*, Vol. 4, No. 47 (November 22, 1993), p. 804.
7. Ibid., p. 803.
8. Quoted in Dana Priest, "U.S. Use of Force in Haiti 'Not Ruled Out,' " *The Washington Post*, October 18, 1993, p. A13.

CHAPTER 9

1. Quoted in Robert Maass, *UN Ambassador* (New York: Walker and Company, 1995), p. 33.
2. Quoted in David Ottaway, "U.S. Presses Balkan War Tribunal," *The Washington Post*, January 7, 1994, p. A14.
3. "Bosnia in Light of the Holocaust: War Crimes Tribunal," *U.S. Department of State Dispatch*, Vol. 5, No. 16 (April 18, 1994), p. 210.
4. Statement Before the UN Security Council, *U.S. Department of State Dispatch*, Vol. 5, No. 21 (May 23, 1994), pp. 327-328.
5. Quoted in Elaine Sciolino, "New U.S. Peacekeeping Policy De-emphasizes Role of the U.N.," *The New York Times*, May 6, 1994, p. A7.
6. "Shared Resolve in Restoring Democracy in Haiti," p. 554.

7. Peter Maass, p. 272.
8. CBS, "60 Minutes," February 9, 1997.
9. Quoted in Barbara Crossette, "U.N. Council Unanimous in Condemning Iraq Move," *The New York Times*, October 17, 1994, p. A10.

CHAPTER 10

1. Quoted in Barbara Crossette, "Albright Makes Her U.N. Post a Focal Point," *The New York Times*, November 25, 1994, p. A14.
2. Quoted in Julia Preston, "U.N. Envoy Albright Emerges as Administration's 'Straight Talker,' " *The Washington Post*, October 14, 1994, p. A34.
3. Ibid.
4. Ibid.
5. Quoted in Robert Maass, *UN Ambassador*, p. 35.
6. Quoted in Richard Z. Chesnoff, "Clinton's Gung-Ho Voice at the U.N., *U.S. News and World Report*, February 13, 1995, p. 62.
7. Quoted in John Goshko and Daniel Williams, "U.S. Policy Faces Review by Helms," *The Washington Post*, November 13, 1994, p. A11.
8. "Advancing American Interests Through the United Nations," *U.S. Department of State Dispatch*, Vol. 6, No. 8 (February 20, 1995), p. 127.
9. Quoted in "Albright, in a Barnard Address, Sees a Trend to U.S. Isolationism," *The New York Times*, May 17, 1995, p. B8.
10. "The United Nations at 50: Renewing the Vision," *U.S. Department of State Dispatch*, Vol. 6, No. 27 (July 3, 1995), p. 536.
11. Quoted in Crossette, "Albright Makes Her U.N. Post a Focal Point," p. A14.
12. Quoted in Barbara Crossette, "U.N. Chief Chides Security Council on Military Missions," *The New York Times*, January 6, 1995, p. A3.
13. Quoted in John M. Goshko, "U.N.'s Normal Decorous Diplomatic Discourse Takes Beating in Dispute," *The Washington Post*, December 16, 1995, p. A30.
14. Ibid.

15. "Fourth World Conference on Women: U.S. Efforts To Promote Equal Rights for Women," *U.S. Department of State Dispatch*, Vol. 6, No. 36 (September 4, 1995), p. 676.
16. Quoted in Cindi Lieve, "Why Women's Rights Are Foreign Policy," *Glamour*, October 1995, p. 161.

CHAPTER 11
1. Quoted in Sciolino, "Madeleine Albright's Audition," p. 66.
2. Quoted in ibid.
3. "The UN: What's in It for the U.S.?," *U.S. Department of State Dispatch*, Vol. 7, No. 11 (March 11, 1996), p. 104.
4. John M. Goshko, "U.N. Search to Begin for Top Position," *The Washington Post*, November 12, 1996, p. A12.
5. Quoted in Steven Erlanger, "Selection for Secretary of State Is Praised by Helms and Others," *The New York Times*, December 6, 1996, p. B6.
6. Quoted in Sciolino, "Madeleine Albright's Audition," p. 87.
7. Quoted in Elaine Sciolino, "State Secret of the Day? Pick a Name," *The New York Times*, November 24, 1996, p. A22.
8. Transcript of presidential press conference, *CNN-Time* All Politics Web Site, December 5, 1996.
9. Ibid.
10. Jim Hoagland, "The Problem Is Not the Choices But the Chooser," *The Washington Post*, December 6, 1996, p. A31.
11. Quoted in Charles Trueheart, "Security Lineup Praised Abroad," *The Washington Post*, December 7, 1996, p. A10.
12. Owen Harries, "Madeleine Albright's 'Munich Mindset,' " *The New York Times*, December 19, 1996, p. A29.
13. Quoted in Cooper and Liu, p. 24.
14. Quoted in Nancy Gibbs, "The Many Lives of Madeleine," *Time*, February 17, 1997, p. 58.

CHAPTER 12
1. A.J.P. Taylor, *The Second World War* (New York: Paragon Books, 1975), p. 148.

2. Eugen Kogon, *The Theory and Practice of Hell*, translated by Heinz Norden (New York: Berkley Books, 1958), p. 310.
3. Quoted in Erlanger, "Albright Grateful for Her Parents' Painful Choices," *The New York Times*, February 5, 1997, p. A8.
4. Quoted in Dobbs, p. 18.
5. Quoted in Erlanger, "Albright Grateful for Her Parents' Painful Choices," p. A1.
6. WAMU radio interview, March 27, 1997.
7. Quoted in Frank Rich, "The Albright Question," *The New York Times*, February 19, 1997, p. A19.
8. Ibid.
9. Quoted in Roger Cohen, "Of Czechs and Jews and the Blinding of Memory," *The New York Times*, February 12, 1997, p. A4.
10. Quoted in Frank Rich, "Albright Comes Home," *The New York Times*, February 26, 1997, p. A23.
11. Ibid.
12. Press Release, Office of the Spokesman, U.S. State Department, July 13, 1997.
13. Quoted in Steven Erlanger, "Albright at Shrine to Victims of Nazis," *The New York Times*, September 11, 1997, p. A12.

CHAPTER 13
1. "Building a Bipartisan Foreign Policy," *Vital Speeches of the Day*, Vol. LXIII, No. 13, April 5, 1997, p. 386.
2. Quoted in "Secretary of State Elevates Women's Issues," *The Hartford Courant*, March 25, 1997, p. 2.
3. *The Christian Science Monitor*, February 25, 1997, p. 1.
4. PBS, "Newshour," March 6, 1997.
5. "Why Bigger Is Better," *The Economist*, February 15, 1997, p. 23.
6. Press Release, Office of the Spokesman, U.S. Department of State, July 15, 1997.
7. "For the Middle East, Peace Is the Only Answer," *U.S. Department of State Dispatch*, Vol. X, No. XX (September 11, 1997), p. 11.
8. Ibid.

9. Quoted in Steven Erlanger, "Albright Says She Found 'Tattered' Mideast Situation," *The New York Times*, September 16, 1997, p. A6.
10. Press Release, Office of the Spokesman, U.S. Department of State, September 30, 1997.
11. Press Release, Office of the Spokesman, U.S. Department of State, February 1, 1998.
12. PBS, "Newshour," February 23, 1998.

CHAPTER 14
1. Quoted in David L. Marcus, "Albright's First Year Earns Her Star Billing," *The Boston Globe*, January 11, 1998, p. A12.
2. NBC, "Meet the Press," October 26, 1997.
3. Ibid.
4. Press Release, Office of the Spokesman, U.S. Department of State, December 18, 1997.
5. Press Release, Office of the Spokesman, U.S. Department of State, January 28, 1998.

INDEX